WHERE
LIBERALS GO
TO DIE

THE END OF LET'S PRETEND

WHERE LIBERALS GO TO DIE

THE END OF LET'S PRETEND

JAMES T. EVANS

Commonwealth Publishing

To
my father
THOMAS BYRON EVANS
whose disaffection for nonsense
shaped my life
far more than
he can ever know

A portion of this text was originally published in *The Houston Post.*

LIBRARY OF CONGRESS CATALOG CARD NUMBER 94-94104

ISBN 0-9640388-0-3

First Edition   94 95 96   5 4 3 2 1

Tough Questions℠ and Insensitivity Training℠ are service marks of Commonwealth Publishing, Inc.

Edited by Rose Marie (Rosie) Walker
Cover design by Gateway Graphics, Inc.
Printed in the United States of America

From 1934 until 1954, one of America's most popular radio shows was a weekly presentation of fairy tales. During the show, the host invited children to let go of reality and imagine a world in which people were filled only with good thoughts and everything would be just perfect.

The name of that radio show was *Let's Pretend.*

CONTENTS

INTRODUCTION

This is one hell of a book, and I guarantee you've never read anything like it before. Why? Because *Where Liberals Go To Die* is about you. It's about your phenomenal power to take control of this country and help America be everything you dream that it can be. When you get a handle on the power of the truth, the pride that comes from taking responsibility for everything in your world, the warmth that flows from honoring the small virtues of life, then—

You will have your own X-ray vision to see through liberal nonsense.

You will have not just the right but the power to ask Tough Questions.

You will have the freedom to tell the truth as you see it—to be insensitive.

You will have an alarm system that will go off every time you get lied to by the government, the media, public education, and the liberal bureaucrats who run our country like their own private playground.

You will know how to shoot down the phony moral superiority of your liberal neighbor, co-worker or brother-in-law.

You will learn that liberals don't even believe the nonsense that they are force-feeding us and our children.

And you will never again go into an argument with a liberal at a disadvantage.

If you still have a liberal streak, stick with me. If you really believe that nonsense, a little preaching from a fully-recovered liberal won't hurt you. But I warn you, I am going to tell you the truth. And some of it will really hurt—especially the part about how hypocritical liberalism is. Let me tell you what pulled me back from the brink.

In 1980, I ran a campaign for a local Democrat—a pretty good fellow. But putting up with all of the pretensions and demands of dozens of special interest groups was wearing me down. I began to wonder if the bleeding hearts believed any of the tax and spend, do-gooder stuff they were peddling.

I got my answer one Saturday when an extremely liberal politician stopped by my house unannounced.

The politico asked "are you alone?" I was. The liberal kept pushing. "Are you sure there is no one here? No girlfriend; no housekeeper; no plumber?" Finally convinced there was no one else around, the liberal asked "Is your third floor soundproof?" It was, so we trudged up there. Then a strange look came over the politico's face, and a scream came out. The lefty shrieked, "Nigger! Nigger! Nigger! Nigger! Nigger!" Then hysteria was followed with a long sigh—a satisfied, sexual-sounding groan. My jaw dropped in shock. Then the Democrat said, "If I never see another conniving, lying greedy black preacher again in my life, I can die happy."

That was it. My eyes were opened to the charade of liberal caring and sincerity.

And that was step one in my personal twelve-step program for dealing with power-mad liberals. It was like a punch in the gut. I knew that my days as a Democrat were numbered.

And that is what this book is really about—how I made the long journey from a paid liberal organizer and student strike leader to a fully-recovered liberal.

If you are a lifelong conservative, if you were born reasonable, congratulations and thanks. Keep reading. America will catch up with you.

But if you are a liberal who picked this book up on the sly and sneaked it home in your Gucci knapsack, I know why you did it. Somewhere in your heart you know that what you say you believe in is a lie. You know what your liberal philosophy has done to America. And you know that if the entire liberal agenda were ever implemented, you wouldn't be able to live here.

You are looking for a way out. You are looking for the graveyard of ideas whose time has come and gone. You've come to the right place, because I know Where Liberals Go To Die.

They die in their own hearts when they face the truth.

• They die when they drive by the neighborhood school that gave them a real education and see the gang graffiti and concertina wire on the fence.

• They die when they talk to their daughters about dignity and self-respect and realize they sound just like Dan Quayle talking about Murphy Brown.

• They die when they hear a rap song about raping women and killing police officers and know that they are too cowardly to say "This has to stop!"

• They die when they are passed over for promotion to meet a racial quota and then try to explain to their kids that skin color doesn't matter.

• They die when they try to explain sexual responsibility to their own kids who know how the old man and the old lady idolize unmarried celebrities and their bastard children.

• They die when they say we must send U.S. troops to stop the holocaust in Bosnia, Rwanda and Haiti and yet can't forget that they spat on our own war-weary Vietnam vets.

But I have hope for the future, and so should you. This is America. We know how to learn from our mistakes. I grew up a Southern Baptist, and I still believe in redemption of the human spirit and forgiveness of sin. But there can be no atonement for the liberal destruction of America's values until we all come clean about what has been going on. And not just the liberals, either.

We conservatives got fat and complacent and let our guard down. Look what we let them do to our schools. We have to take our share of the responsibility. So let's get started.

Where Liberals Go To Die is not just a book. It is a program, a way of life.

It is about telling the truth.

It is about asking Tough Questions.

It is about taking responsibility for your own life.

It is about America.

CHAPTER 1

WHERE LIBERALS GO TO DIE

He who expects gratitude has not conferred a favor.
—Seneca

Once upon a time, good people saw pain and believed that they could ease it. They saw ideas grown rigid and unforgiving. They said "The status quo does not work, and we will change it." They represented what was good about what was once called liberalism. They actually thought things could be better. And they threw themselves into what came to be called "The Movement."

Those people were us—the children of the Sixties and Seventies. Most all of that wonderful philosophy is gone now—if it ever really existed.

From self-conscious idealism we moved directly to self-indulgent self-righteousness. And from there to self-delusion. The legacy of the Nineteen Sixties. It is time for us to stop pretending and to tell the truth about what we—the leaders of The Movement—were really up to. We betrayed the True Believers.

We used them. It was not a pretty story then. Where it has led our nation is a national tragedy. Here it is.

BLAME IT ON THE SIXTIES

All the supposed selflessness of what is now being called liberalism is just self-indulgent romanticism.

I should know. In the Nineteen Sixties, I was a leader of radical students. And my comrades and I were far from altruistic. We expected rewards for our noble efforts. We demanded respect from our fellow liberals for fighting the good fight. That came first. And, way down deep in our hearts, we expected the beneficiaries of our largesse to appreciate and acknowledge us with gratitude—not by saying thank-you, but by agreeing with us absolutely and by living according to our supposed ideals.

You see, we convinced American young people that we possessed *The Answer*. A lot of our generation grew up in a background of fundamental religious absolutism, whether Catholic, Jewish, Southern Baptist or Holy Roller. So when we denounced religion, we all had a vague but serious empty spot where our souls used to be. Liberal thought became our god, our gospel and the one true way. So, when we led them to Mississippi, the ghetto or anyplace else where humanity cried out for our guidance, we engaged the forces of evil with a zeal that would have thrilled any missionary forcing brassieres on Tahitian women.

The downtrodden upon whom we bestowed our wisdom had the good sense or instinct to appear to cling to our new god. So we announced that they were just like all of us—except their houses weren't as nice.

Years passed. Then came the time of reckoning. Some of us realized that the liberal religion—like all the other gods we had followed—was more clay feet than halo. We found that we could not make up the truth and its consequences. Ultimately we found that playing *Let's Pretend* felt good, but that it was not an adequate substitute for reality.

ROCKET SCIENTISTS

For example, a young developer decided that if he could provide adequate housing to the poor—since we had pronounced that they already shared all of our attitudes and values—they would become just like us. The rest of their lives would be dandy and all of their children would be rocket scientists. Subsistence housing was not his forte, however, so his low-income housing included lofts, clawfoot bathtubs, shiny hardwood floors, decks, nifty lighting effects and fancy redwood mailboxes.

The tenants ate the buildings from top to bottom. They raised goats in the bathtubs. They sold the mailboxes and light fixtures. They knocked out the windows for pure joy and jammed things down the toilets under circumstances too bizarre to describe. They dumped dirty diapers in their neighbors' yards and repaired old cars in the fern garden. Then they called the developer in the middle of the night to complain about these self-inflicted injuries. The liberal young developer began to suffer disquieting second thoughts about saving the world through architecture.

What we did next was worse than just stupid. It was social disaster. We proclaimed that it might take more than neat housing to make the poor and downtrodden just like us. It might take jobs just like ours. However, the average poor minority student didn't have the tools to tackle mechanical engineering at the college level. So we insisted that being unqualified, poor and downtrodden be declared the equivalent of being smart and capable. This worked okay until the professor gave the first test and asked the first question. Then we declared that the tests were racist—that $Pi =$ 3.1416+ was a vicious plot contrived by white capitalist pigs to keep the poor of the world under their boot. The laws of physics and chemistry were also a political plot. So if the token students didn't pass, not only the professor but the whole system was oppressive and unworthy of continued existence. Ultimately, a whole bunch of these flawed scholars got loose in the job market with predictable results.

THE WALL

Most of my liberal friends still have very real, practical

problems with the notion of affirmative action for brain surgeons and airline pilots. Sooner or later, all liberals hit this wall.

Their next stop depends on whether they notice they have run out of logic or whether they lie to themselves about it. Here are the obvious alternatives:

1. *VIOLENT RESPONSE.* Irving Kristol said "A neoconservative is a liberal who has been mugged."

These liberals on the run can turn really nasty and overdo their conservatism with the same misguided zeal that made their liberalism so obnoxious. With time, however, they do tend to mellow out and become useful members of society.

2. *MODERATE RESPONSE.* Some people drift away from liberalism for the same reason people wander away from fraternity parties. They get older, wiser and busier. The need to survive and feed the kids tends to put a stop to liberal dithering. Others decide the whole philosophy either doesn't make much sense or isn't an effective way to reach its stated goals. And some old liberals just get bored.

3. *THE SHIP IS SINKING. WHAT WE NEED IS A BIGGER SHIP.* This is the clarion call of a truly dangerous group of liberals. Upon realizing deep in their souls that not even the Ku Klux Klan could have come up with a better long-term program to get people to hate each other, they refuse to admit the truth—especially to themselves. You have a boatload of people sailing off the edge of the world. And nobody on board will change course. Doing so would require admitting they had been wrong. So they explain the rejection of liberalism by claiming they haven't been liberal enough. "What we need are more ships full of more people and more edge of the world to sail off of."

TICKETS TO HELL

Unfortunately, the only way to staff a ship with Hell as its scheduled destination is to shanghai people off the streets. Since it is hard to force a person to be liberal or anything else philosophically, the job is done by the magician's favorite tool—sleight of hand. Lead people in small, seemingly reasonable steps toward a result that could never be sold if described fully in advance. *Tickets to Hell for All You Can Pay* is nobody's idea of a catchy marketing slogan. Instead, let's use affirmative action to produce airplane mechanics out of folks who cannot read, then enforce union rules until we have pilots who can't read either. Seem strange? Read your newspaper and notice how many things truly do not make a bit more sense than this.

We need to watch out for those liberals in the last category. Not all liberals have found a place to die. The bigger-boat crowd has congregated in Congress, governmental bureaucracies, social welfare agencies, ladies' tea rooms and more university administrations and faculties than you can count. A lot of these old liberals are bitter over the exposure of their failed philosophy. And a bitter man at the wheel of a ship—who wants to make a point more than he wants to make it home—is a terrible insurance risk.

Remember, not all liberals have gone gently into that good night. When you run into someone who has ideas that seem really high-minded and vaguely plausible but who wants you to pay for it while he runs it, you have probably cornered one. So, an occasional glance under your bed might not be a bad idea.

What to do with the lingering entrenched results of so many years of liberal *Let's Pretend* is what this book is all about.

But to repair the grievous damage to our culture, we must start our salvage operation where human beings learn their culture—at home.

CHAPTER 2
THE STARTING POINT

Just doing my job, man.
—Your Kid

THE CONVERSATION

"Dad, I'm sixteen now and my instincts tell me it is time for me to learn the rules and get ready to leave home. What's it gonna take for me to get you to do your part of the job?"

Dad reads the paper inertly.

"Okay Dad, I'll rebel if I have to so you'll get off your butt and show me some authority. What's it gonna take?"

No response.

"Okay, how about if I dye my hair purple?"

Dad finally responds. "Oh, that's okay son. You know we're liberals."

"All right, what if I shave my head, paint it and poke a bone through my nose?" goes the kid.

"Oh, that's all right, son. You know we wouldn't want to stifle your creativity. After all, we're dedicated liberals. We've never asked you to obey any rules at all."

"Well, all right you son of a bitch. What if I just blow your damned brains out?"

We think our kids are unemployed, but they are not. They have a bigger job than we do and they work at it 24 hours a day. At the dinner table, in school, playing and especially while driving us crazy. The crazy-driving part is the most important: that's where they are learning the fine points of survival. The most important job in the world. If they are successful, our children get our job; actually surviving as adults.

How they learn to survive is by learning the rules—the rules of the house, the rules of the school, the rules of the other kids, the rules of society. They learn what they can and cannot get away with in a bewildering variety of circumstances. If they learn the rules well, they turn into adult human beings with a reasonable chance of living successful lives.

You can make your kid's job easier or you can make it almost impossible. Kids learn rules by being subjected to them, the same way you learned your job. Just as when your boss gave you orders and critiqued your performance, your kid needs to be given a job and told how he's doing. You wouldn't put up with a job where you never knew what you had to do to get your work done. But your kid doesn't have the option of quitting his job just because you are a lousy boss. So give him a break. Tell him what's expected. Reward a job well done.

Most kids never have to threaten to shoot a liberal weenie parent. But more and more kids aren't learning the rules of survival at home. And the rules they are learning would scare the hell out of you.

SURVIVAL

You have probably worried quite a bit about survival. Am I going to flunk out of college? Am I going to get fired? Am I going to make the car payment? Am I going to eat next week? Am I going to be an old maid? Time and success take our minds off survival. But just have a near-miss collision in your car and see what you think about first. It won't be about whether your socks match or how you rank in the social register.

We don't talk about it much, but survival is what drives our lives. Watch your co-worker who is falling apart in a sales meeting and guess what he is thinking about. Death, in one form or another. When things get tight enough, every thought goes out the window except survival. Now, take your mind off self-preservation. Think about the survival of your family. What would you do if a thug kicked down your door and threatened your loved ones? Survival—pure and simple.

Now make a really big jump. Think about what it would be like if your country didn't exist anymore. What if it didn't survive? Now think about your country still being here but being different. What if you couldn't go see a friend in the next town without a permit? What if your family doctor weren't on the government's approved list? What if you weren't free to stand up and say what you think for fear of who might hear and what might happen to you? What if America weren't America any more? What if it perished from the earth?

This is about survival, just as much as pulling your drowning kid out of the deep water.

HUMAN NATURE

Common sense says we do what it takes to survive. But common sense has gotten a bad rap in America. The Democrats in the White House and in Congress have officially abandoned survival, the basic driving force of nature, as our guiding national principle. We as a nation have gotten so fat and satisfied that we have adopted other standards. Some of them are good—such as fair play and equal opportunity. But the liberals in Washington pretend they can outsmart human nature. They have told our country they can guarantee that everyone will not only survive but succeed, regardless of their contribution. But the liberal Democrats cannot deliver unearned success any more than the Communists could. "From each according to his abilities; to each according to his needs!" doesn't work.

MORNING AFTER

The people of the Soviet Union tried out this theory at gunpoint and enjoyed about as much of it as they could stand. They discovered that a system built on a faulty view of human nature cannot endure. It cannot assure the survival of its subjects. The Russians found out the hard way that a man will work harder to feed his family than he will to get a medal for meeting a factory quota. A gold star is cold comfort on a freezing night. Yet still the Democrats in this country are undeterred.

They have given us affirmative action, social promotions in school, and soon, if they have their way, socialized medicine for the proletariat. We know it doesn't work, just as the East Germans knew it didn't work. We know that everything has a price tag. We know that when the slacker eats for free, a taxpayer goes without lunch. We know that at the end of the binge comes the morning after.

The addict finally hits bottom. The gambler loses the rent and the family gets evicted. The cheating spouse comes home one night to an empty house. The drunkard wakes up in jail. The sinner faces an eternity without hope. And each one cries out for one last chance. And each of them, sooner or later, stands in front of the mirror and stares at the truth.

And one morning after, I saw the man in my mirror. I saw a man who had lived and grown fat on *Let's Pretend*. A man who had traded everything that was precious about America for his chance to trade in power. A chance to be somebody at any price; to tell people how to live their lives. I saw the face of my own *Let's Pretend* liberality hardened into intolerance for any who objected to my dictates for the future. I saw the face of a liberal fascist. And I began to die inside.

I knew then where liberals go to die.

Liberals go to die at the end of the road I call *Let's Pretend*—a road that ends at everyman's mirror of simple, obvious truth. This mirror reveals the wreckage done to our political system, our social and cultural institutions. And finally, it reveals the tattered remains of our self-respect.

Every liberal carries his own mirror in his soul.

He dies a little when his mirror reveals a 16-year-old crack mother living on welfare. And he knows he helped make it possible.

He dies a little more when he sees a homeless psychotic babbling to his own demons. And he knows that liberal policies destroyed the only home that man had ever known.

He dies when he sees the body of a 14-year-old gang member. And he knows his liberal taste destroyed the discipline that could have taught a young man how to survive and be a good American.

The liberal sees the Menendez brothers, who butchered their parents for their inheritance. Then he sees a jury trained on a diet of Donahue that can see those murderers only as victims, not as humans who must bear responsibility for their own evil. And some-place in that liberal heart, reality takes hold. A fear of a world in which no one is responsible for his own deeds.

And somewhere deep in that mirror, the liberal sees the dim reflection of an America that slips away, and hears the tramping of the boots that always follow the abandonment of the individual citizen as the basis of society.

Some will close their eyes to what they see. For to see the truth means condemnation to a liberal's idea of hell—a place where everyone has to mind their own business. Regardless of the cost, they slavishly lie about human nature and continue to tinker with the rules of survival.

And the survival they are fiddling with is not merely their own. It is yours and that of your children.

CHAPTER 3

SURVIVAL

Staying alive. Staying alive.

—Saturday Night Fever

When a baby animal is born, it has only two things going for it: instincts and the ability to learn. It has the instinct to feed itself and to crawl to the water like the self-sufficient turtle. Or it has the instinct to get its parents to feed it, like the helpless baby bird. Both baby creatures then learn quickly, from nature or parents, or they are dead animals.

That is the Law of the Jungle, Article One. Nature does have a system and animals learn it or else. Animal parents know nature's law instinctively.

Wild animals raised in captivity, however, like human children raised without rules, experience an artificial environment. They adapt to a false reality and are unfit to survive in the real world. Human parents who won't feed their children are considered child abusers. Those who won't teach their children the real, stay-alive rules of this world are abusers, too, only a lot more subtle. And they get invited to more wine and cheese parties. Most parents who won't teach their kids the rules they need for survival have chosen to live in a *Let's Pretend* world. It is more fashionable and less trouble for the permissive parents, but the end of *Let's Pretend* will be a jolting reality for these ill-prepared children.

THE BOOMERS

Most of the parents of the Baby Boomers had a pretty good grasp on survival, having had a Depression and World War II to contend with. But they forgot that living close to survival is what turned them into pretty good people. So they decided they didn't want their children to suffer the burdens they had endured. That desire for life to be easier for their children, coupled with their own desire to enjoy their hard-earned luxury, endowed our generation—The Boomers—with a scary and limited understanding of survival.

Our generation, having missed most of the lessons of survival, began to tinker with the culture of America. Oh, we did it for a lot of reasons—a few noble but most not. Having been poorly trained in what really works, we overlooked some fundamental points. For instance, every sailboat can, to some extent, roll with the waves. However, there is a point at which the boat can no longer right itself, so it capsizes. Every good skipper knows that point, especially if he has ever capsized or come dangerously close to it. Our generation, having missed some of the crucial lessons of survival, had no idea our culture could capsize. So we took dangerous risks and ultimately swamped our national capability for social survival. Then, sensing the mess we were making, we turned nasty and declared the boat was still afloat. Anyone who disagreed did so at his own peril.

This book is about the crazy political and cultural system that liberal Democrats have bought into since the Nineteen Fifties and fallen in love with since the Nineteen Sixties.

It is also about the instinct for survival in the face of a bad idea gone into business for itself. This is no longer a matter of sloppy-thinking fringe groupies.

Now the loose thinkers are in the White House and are discovering the principles of state power.

Liberal Fascism

What we have on our hands now can only be called fascism. Liberal fascism. Liberal fascism is not the textbook fascism of state control of private ownership—yet—but rather the fascism of imposing one group's thoughts on all others. An *Il Duce* in a fancy uniform isn't necessary to have a fascist regime. All that is required is the desire of an elitist minority to impose its will on the majority. You measure fascism by its methods and results, not by its trappings. You also measure fascism by its ability to subvert an entire nation away from its inborn sense of what is good for that nation.

CHAPTER 4

NATIONS

Anyone driving coast to coast can see the country.
To see the nation you have to stop and talk to the
people.

—The Author

A country is a place. It has borders and rivers, highways and
wheat fields, cities and forests. You can find a country on a map.

A nation, however, is not the same as a country. A nation is
the contents of a country; what makes a place more than just a
place. It includes the people, but people live and die and are forgotten. A nation is actually defined by boundaries and walls you
may not be able to see, but that nonetheless can be sensed.

For instance, the Jews are one of the longest-surviving nations
on earth. During most of its existence, the Jewish Nation has not
had a country, no land of its own, no physical boundaries. But
because it had no physical walls, it has remained a mighty nation
by virtue of its unseen walls. Those walls are its culture.

Most people have no idea what "culture" is. They either think
it is music and art or white wine and Perrier. Those aren't culture.

They are artifacts and social doodads. Culture is how people survive—the collection of their traits, beliefs, habits, rules, mores, taboos and non-governmental laws and agreements that allow a group of people to live together and prosper. It is the rules they actually live by—the deals a group and its members make among themselves, often without even realizing they have done so.

Every culture has a collection of these characteristics. Some work well. Some don't work worth a damn. The culture of the Roman Empire allowed a small city-state to rule the world and to build the mightiest physical walls ever known. You can see them today in National Geographic under the section called Roman Ruins. As for the remains of Roman culture, it is an unrecognizable mishmash. There are good reasons why the Roman Country and the Roman Nation both fell. However, those reasons had little to do with the ferocity of the barbarians. Rome's physical walls turned to ruins only after the walls of its culture went completely and absolutely to hell. The Romans didn't enforce their cultural rules and, in fact, diluted them until they couldn't even recognize them or remember who they were as a people. Alvin Toffler may have been thinking of the Romans when he observed that culture is like raspberry jam. The further you spread it, the thinner it gets.

By contrast, the Jews didn't have any physical walls worth mentioning, but they survived because their unseen walls were impregnable. They had no choice. The Jews never had the luxury of getting too far from survival, so they had to stick together and respect and reinforce their culture. If they had not, there would be no Jews at all. Because they had no tangible walls and no country of their own, the Jews used what they had—themselves and the rules they had agreed to play by. As they became totally dependent on one another and on the group, the wrath of their enemies only made stronger their nation's unseen walls. Because they knew and honored the rules of their own culture, the Jews survived. Consequently, today there is a powerful Jewish nation all over the globe, not just in the place called Israel.

Now, this fluff that every man hates a wall is exactly that. Every human being, every country and every nation love walls— seen and unseen—because without them we cannot survive.

Our walls are freedom. Freedom from whatever would take away whatever we think our freedom is. Even kneejerk liberals still lock their doors at night.

America has always had a tough, resilient culture, partly because it included a little bit of everything from everywhere. Through it all, first we considered ourselves Americans and we stuck together. But now, for a lot of reasons, we focus not on our similarities but on our differences. New immigrants are pouring into this American country who refuse to join the American nation. Liberal Democrats encourage the internal isolation of these newcomers. Traditional American values are passé, they have decreed; therefore, that which is anything else must be better. Consequently, instead of blending in the best aspects of other cultures, we have developed a fatal attraction for the parts that work the worst and are the least compatible with who we all are. As the notion of a common language and common culture is destroyed by those who glorify anything different, the notion of an "American people" may slide into history.

Meanwhile, we are hanging on to a culture that has served us well. A culture built on the American virtues of independence, self-reliance and personal responsibility. But if we don't pay attention to the unseen walls that define our culture—not as they now are but as they used to be—the America of our future will not be one we recognize. While the values that have kept us alive and well are being dismantled, we are watching the process with only a disconnected interest. The dismantlers have ordered us to be "tolerant" or be branded as bigots. But the tolerance they sell is a one-way street. In the name of ill-defined tolerance and Political Correctness, we have become the enemy of the very things that keep us alive. The rules of our culture.

What is sad is that we aren't even the victims. We are the volunteers. Could we be willing to give away our culture without a struggle because we have so little understanding of how it really works?

CHAPTER 5

HOW CULTURE ACTUALLY WORKS

Gravity is the best friend you ever had. It never lied
to you and it never let you break the rules — not even
once.

—The Author

When American scientists invented the first computers, they looked for parallels in human thought process. After all, we were the only more or less thinking examples available.

Now, in our increasingly desperate attempts to figure out how humans work, we are going back to the very computers we made in our own image. Just what cultural rules can we learn from these machines that first learned from us?

An unplugged computer is only a box of wires and lights. It doesn't "know" whether it is a Macintosh or an IBM. For that matter, it doesn't even know it isn't a toaster. When you turn your computer on, the only thing it can do is look for its system file, which tells it what kind of device it is—who it is, in fact.

The system file tells the computer what language to speak, what symbols to deal in and how to communicate with its other components. The system file reports how fast and powerful the machine is, how much memory it has, how many jobs it can do at the same time, and what its limitations are. The system file also tells the computer what rules it must obey—that two plus two equal four, that the P key means the letter P.

The system file tells the computer how to survive and how to succeed.

Only then can the computer look for a program that tells it what specific kinds of work it can do—accounting, graphics or writing a book. The system file "socializes" the box of wires and lights. It teaches the computer the rules. If the computer doesn't obey them, it is broken and either gets repaired or thrown on the scrap heap. The system file is the computer's culture and survival handbook. The computer either abides by the rules of its culture or it is finished.

People work pretty much the same way. Someone who cannot or does not play by the rules of his culture goes on the scrap heap, too—the unrecovering alcoholic, the crack addict, the thief. Some individuals who fail to learn the rules don't come to such a tragic end. They only suffer the slow death of the emotional cripples whose lives are shortened by failure and frustration, or who never quite find the joy and satisfaction that life is all about.

Individual survival demands that you master the rules of your culture. But what happens if the culture itself doesn't work? If the culture doesn't work, then the better you learn the flawed system, the worse your situation becomes. With what the peddlers of *Let's Pretend* have done to our culture, learning it thoroughly is more dangerous than not learning it at all.

IDLE TINKERING

Most societies don't try to re-engineer their cultures to the extent we in the United States have. Most are disinclined to idle tinkering for its own sake. Most societies don't have our luxury for self-destruction because they are still operating right at the edge of survival. That doesn't make the rigidity of the Iranian mullahs a good idea, but at least when they do decide to make a cultural change, you can bet they have given it considerably more thought than we would have. For good or ill, they know the difference between a Muslim theocracy and a hula hoop.

For a showcase of genuine cultural conservatism, the animal kingdom is hard to beat. Creatures never tinker with their culture, so they don't suffer as many casualties to their own silliness as we do. Examples of what looks like compassion abound in wolf packs, elephant herds, pods of dolphin and elsewhere. But if you look at them long enough and hard enough, you will discover animal species are all survival based. Animals seldom forget that their chief job is the survival of their species. You can observe that truth in the way they raise their offspring.

Just like gravity, animals never lie to their kids. And they never let them get away for long with behavior that doesn't work to the benefit of the species.

CHAPTER 6
KIDS: ANIMAL AND HUMAN

You ought to have a license to raise these things.

—The Author

Nature shows fascinate us. We are intrigued by the way animal parents push fledglings out of the nest and run teenage tigers off into the jungle. Animals are truly insightful parents. But we seem to consider their behavior amusing or poignant, so we are not disposed to learn anything from them.

Animal parents spend endless hours teaching their young the rules that will keep them alive. They can get pretty rough with their babies, too. Like drill sergeants, they have no tolerance for bullshit opinions from trainees when life and death are involved. And make no mistake, animal training is all about life and death. Unlike Americans today, animals do not have the luxury of straying very far from survival. If an animal ever forgets what it's all about, suddenly it's not about anything anymore. Nevertheless, animal parents always know when the time has come for their kids to make it or not. If those kids can't play the survival game by the rules, dying is not just their fate, it is their contribution to the species. Survival of the species demands that the halt, the lame and the stupid not reproduce.

As much time as Americans spend watching nature dramas, it is amazing that we don't pick up on the lessons they offer. Animals start out with a pretty firm inventory of instincts, whereas human children are born with few instincts and none of what we adults use in place of instincts—beliefs and culture. We learn the rules of survival from our parents, our families and local society. Teaching kids the rules has been done so effectively throughout America's history that we had come to think the skill was instinctive. Until now. Now, parents seem unable or unwilling to teach their kids. And they sure don't know when to cut them loose.

FLYING ON AUTOMATIC

When the parents fail them, the kids go on automatic. Every parent knows that even before a child is old enough to walk, he's old enough to test the rules. Two-year-olds discover the rules and the urge to break them at the same time. By age 16, kids have elevated violence to the rules to an art form. These kids know instinctively that they must find out the rules and master them quick and hard, or they face a short social life expectancy. That fact of life must be etched into their brains early.

Ultimately, kids will run into rules. If they don't get the instruction at home, they may hit the wall at the hands of a first-rate drill sergeant or a tough employer. Love can turn a street thug into a gentleman caller. Some kids will learn their lesson in prison. Amazingly enough, others, with no help at all, manage to figure things out on their own. And some will learn the perverted rules of the street gang and many will die by them.

MERE STATISTICS

If they don't figure out the rules fairly early, kids will turn into statistics: can't get an education, can't hold a job, can't make a marriage work, can't stay clean and sober. A whole bunch of them won't even figure out how to stay alive. Parents know this, but many of them can't figure out how teaching the rules connects with their own kids. You can see some of these young tyrants in restaurants disrupting everyone else's meal while mommy and daddy gaze on blissfully.

Any self-respecting tiger—operating on instinct alone without the benefit of the great love we supposedly hold for our children—would be run out of the jungle if he handled his job the way many parents do. These slackers are parents who have never enforced, day in and day out, the rules their children know enough to be seeking instinctively. They probably think they are good parents, but they have never taught a cultural right or wrong. They haven't taught their children how to survive. These parents are deadly to their own kids and to society. Do they have no awareness of the effects of their coddling or disinterest?

Kids *are* going to learn rules—at least some kind of rules. But merely teaching rules isn't enough. The rules must be practical, real survival rules. Dumb ones, regardless of how fashionable they may be, are worse than no rules at all. Teaching our kids *Let's Pretend* instead of let's survive is the real root of what's wrong with America.

So what is wrong with America anyway?

CHAPTER 7

WHAT'S REALLY WRONG WITH AMERICA

Better is the enemy of good enough.
—Observation of a Russian cavalry general
when the wings fell off his new airplane

We have quit doing what works and have started doing what might work. That is what is wrong with America. At first blush, this seems like a pretty logical way to make progress. But we better have enough sense to quit doing what might work when it becomes obvious that it won't work. As the stand-up philosopher George Carlin might say, Americans have gotten serious non-sense mixed up with honest bullshit.

Need a vivid example? Think back to the "new math" of the late Nineteen Sixties. In theory, new math was rather intellectually liberating. It was devised so students could learn that there are many ways to approach a problem. If you were fortunate enough to have missed new math entirely, it was a system of counting by eights rather than our traditional system of counting by tens. In reality, new math was just another Sixties practical joke that allowed newly-minted Doctors of Education to persuade legitimate, hard-working educators to retire and hand over the public school systems to people who couldn't even spell and who had no way of telling whether they could count or not.

There is nothing wrong with different numerical bases. Ask anyone who keeps track of eggs by the dozen (base 12), paper by the ream (base 540), or bakers (who think a dozen is 13), or Englishmen who can't agree with anybody on how much ale is in a pint. The bottom line is that change for its own sake—or actually for the profit of those promoting the change—is not necessarily the equivalent of progress. The old Soviet military was well known for its unsophisticated but extremely reliable equipment. The Red Army didn't fiddle with what already worked. As long as most humans have the usual complement of fingers and toes, base ten arithmetic will work just fine for everyone.

So why the fixation on dumb ideas, other than the historical imperative of all civilizations—from the Roman Empire backward and forward—to get dumber with time?

ADRENALINE

There is a simple reason why we keep generating new and worse ideas. When just staying alive is no longer difficult enough to be challenging, we tackle bold new ideas. This is both the luxury and the detriment of not having to worry about getting enough to eat. Ironically, if challenge is what we seek, the dumber and less likely a bold idea is to work, the greater the adventure and the more we fall in love with it.

Pursuing dumb bold ideas is probably explained by the widespread human addiction to our own adrenaline. However, mountain climbers and skydivers tend to be extremely conservative about great new ideas and techniques—especially those advanced by the kind of people who make their living foisting new educational deals off on children too young to notice that their theories don't make any sense. Present any mountain climber with an innovative but untested new rope. Then ask him what he thinks about that kind of excitement.

Whether you buy into the "excitement theory" or the "progressively more stupid theory," a few outstanding examples of "progressive programs" deserve special examination. In the 1970's, "progressive education" faced its first big challenge when kids started flunking out of high school at an even faster rate, despite supposedly sensitive and enriched learning environments. Fortunately for the crafty educators, most Americans are as mystified by educational theories as we are by quantum mechanics. Knowing that all we were likely to notice was how many kids were being graduated, the new educators coming out of the Nineteen Sixties socially promoted kids to the next grade regardless of their academic performance. When pressed, the educators came up with the fast-shuffle justification that letting kids stay with their peers would keep them from dropping out and might result in some incidental learning—perhaps by osmosis or copying from someone else's test paper.

In application, all the social-promotion policy did was postpone the day of reckoning with the illiteracy of our young people. But its virtue, from the liberal educrats' point of view, was that it would take us much longer to figure out what our schools were doing with our money and to our kids. Both the "excitement theory" and the "stupid theory," may have been at work here. As school systems and school kids became progressively more stupid, the prospect of being shot by a 16-year-old certainly made the school day perversely more exciting.

In 1971, the U.S. Supreme Court decided that lining up school kids at a bus stop before dawn so they could go to a school they had never heard of was mandated by the U.S. Constitution. Even the most regressive liberals among today's educators concede that the active involvement of parents and a supportive home environment are essential to learning. Yet a majority of the people to whom we have entrusted our kids not only tolerated years of forced busing, they have considered it an article of faith. The mere suggestion that busing should be carefully scrutinized as an educational policy has always been the quickest way to get thrown out of a Chablis and Brie party.

I suppose the prospect of being dumped into a sea of different and hostile classmates could be educational, much as kicking the neighbor's pit bull could be aerobic. But it has taken 20 years for federal judges and educators to begin to figure out what the dumbest kid in class has known all along. Destroying the links among parents, students, teachers, administrators and neighborhood is a blueprint for disaster. Most Americans now look upon busing—the acid test of liberal progressive education—as kindly as they do a schoolyard child molester. But the progressive peddlers of forced busing have skipped right over "Excuse me!" and gone straight to "Never mind!"

PROGRESS

With the public schools in shambles, "progress" headed for American universities. College students, traditionally ideal-stricken, have always had an exaggerated and skewed sense of fair play. One of the purposes of college education is to bring the student along from his parochial past, into youthful idealism and finally to a realistic view of how things really are. It is no surprise that the shiftlessly-opinionated activists of the Nineteen Sixties laid the foundation for the college admission policies of the Nineteen Eighties and Nineteen Nineties. Under the banner of diversity (say minimum reading and math skills) and tolerance (say anti-intellectual, Politically Correct fascism), students are admitted to our universities more on the color of their skin than the content of their character. At the University of California at Berkeley—traditionally an academically tough and scrupulous campus—only 40 percent of the 1990 freshman class were admitted on the basis of academic merit. The remaining 60 percent were admitted to provide a student ethnic mix that mirrored the population of California.

Even in the face of the obvious, Berkeley's administration bravely maintained their admission policies were not race-based and made good educational sense. Unfortunately, to make its quotas, Berkeley admitted wholly-unprepared minority students who burned out and dropped out at about three times the normal rate. At the same time, Asian students were being turned away because their academic achievement and determination caused them to be over-represented. When Berkeley's administrators devised their quota minimums, they overlooked the effect of quota maximums. Probably the result of figuring it out in new math.

Ignore for the moment the human misery inflicted on deserving scholars excluded and unqualified students admitted then abandoned. The greatest personal damage is done to the minority students who were admitted on merit and who succeeded on drive and will. These real scholars live with the knowledge that they are indistinguishable from the quota students who do not deserve to carry their books. Walking across most university campuses today is like going to a hospital where both the orderlies and the surgeons are called doctor. That may sound egalitarian and probably does a lot for the janitor's self-esteem, but it ought to scare the hell out of the patients.

LITHUANIAN BRAIN SURGEONS

Where we really go crazy is when we decide to mix "progress," "compassion" and national policy.

In 1990, the U.S. Congress passed a new immigration bill. One of its provisions deals with the tide of newly-free Eastern Europeans wanting to try their luck in America. A lot of these folks are skilled craftsmen—machinists, welders and the like—with a history of hard work under tough conditions. It sounds pretty sensible that one of our principal standards for admitting them into the U.S. should be whether we have a shortage of people with their skills.

So why do we allow half a million (give or take, who knows?) Mexicans and Central Americans to walk across the Rio Grande every year without even asking them if they might be Lithuanian brain surgeons trying to sneak around our immigration laws? The only answer to this has to be our longstanding, desperate shortage of people with graduate-level training in Guatemalan peasantry.

It's hard to argue that the average Central American doesn't have a tough life. But what kind of message are we sending when a half-million people a year are given firsthand proof that we either don't care about our laws or perhaps are too stupid to enforce them? Next time you try to have the old "respect for the law" talk with your kid, just pray that his specialty is video games and not immigration policy.

CHAIRMAN MAO

Anyone can see that quotas, social promotions, busing and misplaced compassion don't work. But how many of us are ready to stand up and say "Stop this crap! That's enough of this dumb idea!"? In our desire for things to be other than the way they really are, we have substituted *Let's Pretend* for common sense. We who know what is going on are even starting to pretend that liberals are not playing *Let's Pretend*. Now, there is nothing morally reprehensible about playing pretend, especially with small children. Trying to lie about the facts to grown people, however, can engender some profoundly nasty responses.

Take Mao Tse Tung, the father of Chinese Communism. Mao made some phenomenal marks on world history. He started with a ragtag band of malcontents, led them on the Long March of the 1920's, practiced guerrilla warfare on the Japanese during World War II, and finally overthrew the forces of Gen. Chiang Kai-shek, until then the absolute ruler of China.

Mao made himself a secular god, forcing the Chinese people to read his "Little Red Book," *Quotations from Chairman Mao*, as though it were the Torah, Bible or Koran. But for all his power and self-deification, the Chairman discovered how difficult it is to lie effectively about certain things.

Mao was every bit as good as Adolf Hitler at what is called "The Big Lie." Things like "You are the master race." But Mao carried the lie one step too far with what he called the "Great Leap Forward." There were a number of these leaps. Each leap involved Mao declaring that tomorrow the Chinese people would grow twice as much rice as they had the day before, or that steel production would triple. Chairman Mao tried to pretend his country to greatness and fell on his butt. But the rest of the world wasn't watching, and thus we missed the point.

So we keep playing *Let's Pretend*. We pretend that social promotions work. We pretend that people respect things they get for free. We pretend that self-esteem is more important than self-discipline and character. On and on we pretend.

America must never give up its eagerness to seek better ways to make and do. Without our spirit of curiosity and adventure, all 250-odd million of us would be living within ten miles of Plymouth Rock. But the liberal notion of "Let's all be willing to try some new ideas!" has turned into a liberal orthodoxy that tolerates no criticism of even the most discredited of tired old "progressive" notions. Most of these examples of "progress" seem to have something to do with one minority or another. Most liberal programs pit some minority against some other minority. An emerging scapegoat minority group is middle-class folks with jobs—regardless of their color or race—whose cardinal sin is allegiance to the traditional aspects of American culture.

DIRTY NAMES

If Gallup really knows how to run an opinion poll, more than three-fourths of our fellow Americans can't figure out how we got into this mess. Americans may not be certain what to do about it, but we are becoming very clear that we don't like it. But as citizens, we are the ones who allowed these liberal ped-dlers of dumb ideas to position themselves so that anyone who points out that the liberal emperor is buck nekkid gets shouted down as a bigot.

The word bigot, by the way, has become the switchblade of any liberal Democrat in an argument. This is akin to being called a "counter-revolutionary" by Joseph Stalin or a "Communist" by crazy old Senator Joe McCarthy. Once you have been labeled with one of the trendy dirty names, you are considered such a bad person you aren't even allowed to speak up in your own defense.

Calling someone you disagree with a "racist" is also popular these days. And "sexist" and "homophobe" have become stylish epithets. As a matter of fact, name-calling is becoming the national pastime, especially among the Politically Correct. However, the Politically Correct maintain that minorities cannot be racist even as they throw white students out of their "black theme" dormitories and student unions. For instance, Vassar College held separate blacks-only graduation ceremonies in 1991. But the right to call people dirty names is not reserved only to ethnic minorities. It has become the province of all of the self-proclaimed victims of the world.

"Sixty Minutes" commentator Andy Rooney observed that homosexual practices that lead to contracting AIDS were voluntary assumptions of health hazards, much like smoking, drinking and overeating—a position shared by most of our mothers. That comment led to allegations by an avowed homo-sexual journalist—journalism being one of the last great professions that you don't have to pass a test to get into—that Rooney was also a racist. Nothing in the conversation between Rooney and his interviewer seemed to support the racist allegation, but the journalist apparently figured that anyone who suggested that homosexuals should be responsible for their actions probably held some other pretty offensive views as well.

American liberaldom joined the chorus. CBS immediately pulled him off the air. Somehow the notion of censuring Andy

Rooney for occasionally coming off like a horse's rear offended enough viewers that CBS relented. The network did not relent in time to prevent Rooney from apologizing for something or other that was extremely hard to follow.

But Rooney wasn't alone.

Lecturing as a visiting professor at Vassar, U.S. Sen. Daniel Moynihan was taking a barrage of heckling from the audience. Seems the Democrat Senator was to blame for the liberal laundry list of American evil traits and habits. Moynihan tolerated the heckling for a while, but he finally made the mistake of telling a lady from another country that if she found America so oppressive she was welcome to go home. Bland enough reaction—actually pretty restrained, allowing for the level of abuse she was handing out. But the woman was from Jamaica, so Moynihan was clearly a racist. Whether Moynihan even knew the lady heckler was black did not seem to carry much weight.

The scholars at Vassar decided they didn't like the senator's views and demanded Moynihan be expelled as a guest lecturer. But first, they demanded he deliver a groveling apology. As the intelligentsia at Vassar prepared their indictments, Moynihan got his fill of the Politically Correct. He had the good sense and the integrity not to apologize for a patently non-racist remark. He decided intellectual freedom was no longer a guiding policy at Vassar. He severed his tie to Vassar, in amazement if not disgust.

The Vassar administration never got around to apologizing for their student thugs or their own lapse in teaching their young charges a little civility.

INTELLECTUAL HOODLUMS

"Thug," appropriately enough, derives from an old Indian religious sect known as the Thugees. They would befriend a traveler. Then, once he was comfortable with his new friends, they would kill him in a wild frenzy. Unlike the Politically Correct, the Thugees' mania was at least the result of honest drug abuse and religious lunacy rather than pretentious intellectual self-indulgence.

Once upon a time, one of the reasons people went to college and listened to commentators was to hear viewpoints that might differ from their own. Whether Rooney's and Moynihan's comments were right or wrong, bigoted or not, they certainly qualify for the protection of the First Amendment. If you can't figure out why this whole deal makes you uncomfortable, go rent a video of Adolf Hitler and watch as he explains his ideas on fair play and human relations. In fact, those Vassar women could learn a lot from studying the Hitler Youth as well. Their techniques are similar.

Today's Vassar bosses were Movement groupies in the Nineteen Sixties. Back then, we loved to accuse everyone who disagreed with us of being fascists. We weren't actually talking about a political system with a dictator in a fancy uniform. We just used the word to rail against whomever we were beating up at the moment. We knew our fathers and the college dean had lost their brothers and friends fighting fascism in World War II, so calling them fascists was as good as peeing on their shoes. Incidentally, that was done, too.

If the treatment handed out to Rooney and Moynihan wasn't fascism, it is hard to imagine what else it would look like. That these episodes were displays of liberal fascism should only make them all the scarier. Those two men were run out of town because their lack of Political Correctness made them unfit to be heard. Attacking the speaker's character rather than his message has a long and dishonorable history.

Since liberal escapists are running the campuses now, this kind of obnoxious behavior should not be too surprising. We loved to shout down unpopular speakers in the middle of the Nineteen Sixties free-speech rallies. Shouting down was one of our sacraments. By the early Nineteen Seventies, those of us who organized campus strikes and demonstrations had literally beaten up enough people who tried to disagree with us that we were reduced to bringing in sympathetic leftist shills from other campuses, dressing them in suits, then chasing them off the stage on cue.

LIBERAL FASCISTS

So what's so offensive about letting today's college liberal fascists—faculty, administrators and students—savage anyone who disagrees with them? Well, what was wrong with letting the Nazis beat up on anyone they didn't like?

Simple. The squelching of unpopular thought has always been the cutting edge of totalitarianism. Suppression of free speech and thought by liberal college administrations has gotten so out of hand that even the ACLU has waded into the battle. And this time they have checked in on the side of the good guys.

You could pick up the leaders of Political Correctness and time-warp them back to Berlin in 1936. As soon as they had changed into those nifty brown shirts, you wouldn't be able to pick them out from the rest of the book burners. Hitler would have loved these guys. Anyone who can sell a nation on the idea that free speech is not sacred can sell it a lot of other offensive ideas, too. Problem is, we have forgotten that a nation like America and the culture that makes it great cannot survive without a First Amendment.

We have gotten so far away from the common sense rules of national social survival that we just don't understand how our own culture works anymore and how fragile our freedom is. And we lost our way in the carefree days of our childhood—the Nineteen Fifties.

CHAPTER 8

THE FIFTIES

I want my own Coupe de Ville, let my dad pay the
bill. Yeah man, that's heaven to me.
— Eddie Cochran in *Teenage Heaven*

Americans have always lived pretty close to the edge. If you didn't work hard during the day, you and the family didn't eat that night. During the Great Depression, Americans of all classes went to bed hungry. Middle managers rode boxcars hunting work. Middle-class mothers took in laundry. Elementary students left school to work full time shining shoes to support their infant siblings. With millions of once-prosperous Americans facing starvation, the nation's attention was riveted on survival. The average citizens of most world cultures still live that way. Nonetheless, as tragic as the Depression was, it served to prepare Americans for the utter sacrifice of World War II.

Without your knowing it, being a survivor keeps you in harmony with your culture. During World War II, everyone pulled together for the common good. Everyman and everywoman were expected to carry their share of the load, because doing so was necessary for our nation's survival. The privation of the Great Depression had an unexpected payoff. We were tough enough to dig even deeper into our exhausted national will to go to battle for those facing not mere hunger, but the horrors of genocide.

Then the Allies won the Great War. Suddenly the scarcity of the Great Depression and the hardships of war were fading into memory. The fascist threat to our survival was over—we assumed forever. The mighty industrial base of America didn't need to make tanks and planes any more. Now, we made cars and refrigerators. G.I.'s who had been expecting to return to the simple rural life of their childhood and their ancestors wound up in the big city. They also wound up in a new G.I. home, with a new Chevrolet and new Frigidaire, sitting in front of their very own television set.

FAIR PLAY

Not even that sudden and precipitous fulfilling of undreamt dreams could wipe out our survival-based culture. But it was transformed. Every man doing his share, but not just because the triumph of democracy over the invidious Axis powers (Germany, Italy and Japan) demanded it or because he had a hungry family. He carried his own load because that was the right thing for him to do. It was fair and it was reasonable and most everyone had that unspoken agreement with everyone else, whether they recognized it or not. A line of Biblical proportions had been crossed. Suddenly, America no longer believed in mere survival. Instead, we believed in "fair play." For the first time in history, a conquering nation reached out and lifted up the vanquished. We wrote a new constitution for Japan. The Marshall Plan rebuilt a shattered Europe. We actually learned the lesson of World War One—grinding the loser into the dirt only assures that another war will be fought. Fairness and generosity became part of our national character. And we liked the way it felt.

As fine a concept as fairness is, the disappearance of outright survival as the foundation of American culture during the Nineteen Fifties had two disastrous results. The students of the Nineteen Sixties became the first generation of Americans who grew up free from the Biblical principle that "If a man does not work, he shall not eat." Also, their parents decided to protect their offspring from the deprivation and suffering they themselves had felt in the Depression and during the War.

At the same time, we, as a nation, made ourselves the parents to the entire world. We would protect them and teach them our values, forgetting the Law of Unintended Consequences. As the generosity of our foreign aid drifted into coercion and then out-right bribery, we replaced evil, self-employed megalomaniacs with spoiled brat dictators who were on our payroll. We forgot, once again, how difficult it is to buy friends.

SPOILED ROTTEN

As usual, most of the kids survived their spoiling without damage—at least little that was apparent. The real damage to the children of the Nineteen Fifties was a general diminution of character, which they demonstrated by putting up with the rest of their own generation, both then and now. During the War, if someone wanted to do something stupid, self-indulgent and dangerous to the survival of the group, the rest of the platoon or assembly line promptly kicked him in the ass. But peacetime endeavors, like peacetime armies, run on a looser standard because they are not quite so close to the edge of survival.

A whole generation of parents decided to rewrite the story of their own Depression-scarred childhood by indulging their children. Their kids would have the car they never had, the parties they never went to and the total freedom from all responsibility they never imagined. But they forgot the law of the universe that no one can stand a spoiled child.

Our client nations, just like our spoiled children, never knew when to stop asking for more. And we didn't have the will to say no. Our "ask and ye shall receive" policy was obviously a bad idea, but we Americans decided to damn the survival and full spoil ahead.

Dead ahead to the Nineteen Sixties.

CHAPTER 9
THE SIXTIES

We chanted "Peace and Love" and "Kill the Pigs"
and couldn't even hear the contradiction. In less than
a generation, the groundwork was laid for the rebirth
of fascism.

—The Author

The first college dean whose office was seized by force had the opportunity to alter the course of U.S. history. He could have had us dragged out by the heels then hosed down. The peace and love generation didn't care for that kind of indignity. If he'd really had a mean streak, he would have demanded a serious discussion of our grievances. If he had, the Dean would have discovered a fact beyond his imagination. Few of the would-be radicals had any particular grievances they could articulate, either to the Dean or to us, their self-anointed leaders.

In the late Nineteen Sixties, there were plenty of grievous conditions on college campuses. Campus police kicked down the doors of private, off-campus living quarters looking for "perverts." Dormitory supervisors opened student mail. Local police staked out communes. Overshadowing the entire era was the fear of universal military conscription. A simple disagreement with a dean could lead to expulsion. For hundreds of thousands of healthy young men, the loss of a cherished student draft deferment was a ticket to the bloody Central Highlands of Vietnam. Every 24 hours, the evening news broadcast the carnage; guys our own age, scared, maimed or dying.

But despite these horrors, The Movement didn't capture the Dean's office as a desperate last effort at survival against the oppression that was crushing human liberty. We did it because it was a hoot and a wonderful opportunity to get laid. Even then the trappings of power were a dandy aphrodisiac. Our actions were the outrageously logical outgrowth of the sophomoric tricks students have been pulling on teachers as long as there have been schools.

Yet our wild good time was set against the backdrop of the constant threat of becoming cannon fodder in Vietnam. A draft notice became the defining force in the lives of college students. It dictated what you studied, whether you went to graduate school, when you got married and when you started a family. All of these were elements in preserving and tending the most valuable of all commodities: our stay-out-of-Vietnam deferments.

How did we, the self-styled leaders, get frightened students to fly in the face of their own survival interest? Why were we not afraid of this same fate as we pompously faced down the Establishment? The answers: we considered the True Believers sheep for the fleecing, and we knew we weren't the lambs who would go to the slaughterhouse.

The True Believers had lost the self-righting mechanism of survival—"If we pull this stunt our parents are going to quit writing those checks"—to guide them. For several reasons, we the leadership doubted that the university would kick us out. Perhaps because of the draft or parental pressure, or even a general lack of character on the part of the administrators.

Although there were profound inequities on campus and in the real world as well, they were of little interest to us. Our specialty was the non-negotiable demands. These seldom had any particular authority or importance, but were selected because nobody with any sense at all could possibly accept them under any circumstances. Thus the game would continue.

PROFESSIONAL PROTEST

My fellow opportunists and I flew all around the country helping other protesters determine and state their grievances and demands. After two hours of intense huddling with protest leaders, we would determine that the biggest gripe they could articulate usually involved the dessert selection in the cafeteria or some gibberish about class struggle. There were plenty of real problems, but the protesters just didn't have any idea what they were. They hadn't locked the Dean out of his office for any real philosophical reason. So we would give them our prefab list of grievances and demands. After they memorized our list, we set them loose on an eager press and their dumbstruck Dean.

These were kids whose parents had refused to teach them the rules of survival. So as students they went on automatic pilot, trying desperately to discover what the rules were without even understanding the instincts that drove them. What happened was a total surprise beyond our most optimistic expectations. The Dean declared there really weren't any rules, so we should make up some of our own.

Now why would a man with a hard-earned Ph.D., a responsible position and the respect of his peers act so strangely? We all thought he was crazy for rolling over. We wouldn't have surrendered to anyone like us. We knew our position was pure sophistry, though we didn't know that name for it because we were skipping philosophy classes at the time. We never suspected what had prompted the Dean to adopt such uncontemplated silliness.

Fact was, the Dean, a World War II vet, was still operating under the old culture based on fair play. Consequently, he thought students could only be driven to such extreme action by true desperation over immense issues of survival or, at the very least, fundamental human fairness. So he reacted like most men would to a screaming child. His reflex was to come to the rescue.

But our survival wasn't threatened. Furthermore, we had only the slipperiest grasp on fair play. We were bored! We had no worries about survival, so we could devote our full attention to having a good time.

Along the way we noticed that wielding power was the best time you could have.

PEACE AND LOVE, BROTHER

So you can fully appreciate (or recollect) the culture of that time, go back with me to a commune near a large university. A green freshman enters the room, never having seen any naked and precious few partially-clad coeds. He sees beer, dope, friendly women. He hears "Hey, peace and love, brother. You against the war?" So he asks "What war?" Shortly, he gets stoned, laid and thoroughly re-educated. By the end of the afternoon, he is against the war and whatever else his new family suggests.

Incidentally, the principal point raised against the war heating up in Vietnam was the grim likelihood of our personal selves getting shot at. There were absolutely no cosmic overtones of peace and brotherhood. Only later did we develop an overpowering belief that shooting our yellow brothers in Southeast Asia was so despicable that fundamental morality demanded we prove our manly courage by calling the police nasty names and sticking flowers in gun barrels.

TRUE BELIEVERS

Unlike the concealed but overwhelming cynicism of those of us in at the start of The Movement, many of the later arrivals held sincere beliefs. We called them the True Believers.

We also called them mullets. They would believe anything we told them.

If Vietnam and civil rights hadn't shown up in time, The Movement would have manufactured other deals. After all, this was a movement that began with the moral force of a panty raiding gang following a bad map. It should come as no surprise that we wound up in the administration building instead of the girls' dormitory.

Actually, on campuses, it was pretty easy to round up dedicated converts to almost any belief system that involved a lot of sex, marijuana, beer, group acceptance and high-flung principles. That particular parlay of party favors is a proven hit.

And most students love to go against the flow. In the 1930's, we could have wound up Nazis except for lacking the discipline. We certainly loved our uniforms, insignia and the rituals of our movement—especially our war surplus field jackets.

For all our pretense of democratic communalism, we ran the communes and The Movement on an absolute leader/unquestioning follower hierarchy. So it's not surprising it all turned out to be fascism, although of a whole new strain.

THE CURSE OF THE SIXTIES

Yet the real structural damage to our generation has only become manifest today. Because we got away with making stuff up and having it treated as God's own truth, we lost the ability to tell what was real from what we merely said was so. This is the real *Curse of the Sixties*—a form of moral and political sociopathy. You can see this curse at work in the Clinton White House as scandal follows self-inflicted disaster. The Clintonoids just don't seem to "get it" because they do not understand that there is an "it" to get. Having decreed that something is so, they cannot fathom how it can be demonstrated to be otherwise.

We wound up with free love and nickel beer. Our country wound up with a bunch of self-deluding, junior-grade fascists running loose on campus. Other than the obvious reason that we were having one hell of a good time, why did we do all this?

Easy answer. Power!

Chapter 10

Power

*Power is money and money is power. Power is sex
and sex is power. Power is fame and fame is power.
Power seems to be where it's at.*
                                    —Any Politician in the USA

The biggest problem with being young, bright and having all
the answers was that someone else had all of the power. Freed
from the tedium of staying alive, we wanted power immediately,
not power someday. We called it *Power to the People,* but we
were damned careful to see that the people got nowhere near it.
We, the few dozen student leaders of The Movement, wanted to
seize power for the same reasons the handful of people running
the country wanted to keep it. Power will get you sex, money,
fame and most anything else you want—including more power.

Having read a bit of history, we realized that all revolutions
come down to "us against them." Our takeover plan had two parts.
First, we would contrive new rules and values for American society
that would scare the pants off the ruling class. Then we would
peddle our new dogma to our customers—minorities, the poor

and the perennially disgruntled. But first, we had to recruit a sales force—the most pampered group of students who had ever lived. Ideas and discontent were cheap and plentiful. The real secret was in the organization and staffing. We recruited students with our philosophical bonus package: free love, free drugs, do-it-yourself degree plans, authority-be-damned, and the chance to be consumingly self-righteous. Our advertising department—the folks who spread the word of the coming Revolution—would be the radical entertainers like John Lennon, Bob Dylan and Joan Baez. And the limousine liberals like Leonard Bernstein, Norman Mailer and folks who had inherited every million they had.

Losing any of its power was about as offensive an idea as the Establishment could imagine. Losing it to the downtrodden led by the unwashed was intolerable. All we had to do was offer the poor and minorities everything the Establishment owned and valued. As the brokers of that deal, we were guaranteed to become the new power elite. "Elite" is the operative word in this deal, although we saw ourselves more as poet kings than corporate fat cats. We were big on equality, but we were clear that some of us were a bit more equal. We demonstrated our distinction by flying to demonstrations first class. It added a certain mystique and moral authority to our message of liberation. And the seats were softer.

The supposed beneficiaries of this free lunch—our clients, the downtrodden masses—figured if the pot were only churned enough, something good for them might float to the top. A lot of them weren't necessarily looking for a handout but hoped they might at least get a shot at improving their miserable lots. Like all brokers, we the leaders were in it for the commission.

It has taken a full generation, but our contrived Revolution has prevailed. On January 20, 1993, Bill and Hillary Clinton took possession of the White House. With them they brought a culture shaped by "If it feels good, do it." Our sweet-sounding, fuzzy-think philosophy now has nasty progeny. The chickens have come home to roost. Free love has become sexual license which has begotten a plague of sexual disease and illegitimacy. Free drugs set the stage for a crack-crazed youth culture. Self-created edu-crats have built a public school system in which no one can read, write or spell. Defiance of authority has spawned gang warfare and waves of illegal immigrants. And the cloying self-righteous-ness of a Bill and Hillary Clinton urges America to pretend that none of this is happening.

How could The Movement subvert the national survival culture? Why did the rest of America, the people who pay the bills, go along? How has the Revolution of the Sixties taken over the United States?

The explanation? Tribal survival mechanism kicked in. Since the dawn of time, instinct has dictated that the tribe must be pro-tected. An enemy of the tribe must be killed or co-opted. That

instinctive fear of strangers keeps tribal culture from being cor-
rupted by alien ideas. Coupled with that fear of anything foreign
is the equally powerful fear of any change whatsoever.

This is not ancient history. These tribal reflexes still prevail:
in Bosnia, in Rwanda and in Ireland.

WHO PAID FOR IT

As our movement gained momentum, the nation's political
leaders dealt with their fear of change and outsiders in their usual
manner. First they tried to kill The Movement by putting people
in jail. Draft resisters. The Black Panthers. Radical clergy.

When jail didn't defuse the growing Revolution, the Establishment used its ultimate weapon: money. The American
intelligence community got in bed with us and left a lot of
money on our pillow. We didn't ask who was the whore. We just
did business with each other.

Ordinary Americans, stunned by the gleeful madness on their
doorsteps, found another way to cope. They pretended the Revolution wasn't happening. They tuned it out. Hoped it was just
another passing phase. Prayed that their weird sons and daughters would not disgrace the family.

My fellow Revolutionaries and I—driven by the smell of our
own power disguised by the incense of justice for all—were
secretly tormented by these same fears. Being a bit embarrassed

at how good our lust for power felt, we pretended not to comprehend that all people are different. We chanted universal brotherhood, but we knew better. We knew brotherhood was not universal by noticing how we were treating the women in our own Revolution as servants and sex objects. We had constructed a dogma of peace and equality, but we found it damned hard to live by. The time we spent lying about human differences and pursuing the bogus goals of our Revolution was time stolen from building a more productive and inclusive national culture.

How strange it all became! Chanting and incense did not cure inequality. Equal opportunity was not producing equal results. Individuals were still individuals. Tribesmen still hated strangers. What fell out of apple trees were still apples. Things were not turning out as we predicted.

Any soothsayer whose prophesies don't come true must be nimble and clever.

So, to keep up the pretense of our Revolution, we decreed that fair play and equal opportunity were not enough. We demanded that things had to turn out the way we said they would— even if it defied the laws of nature.

CHAPTER 11
SLOW GAZELLES

*The cheetah is the best friend of the gazelles. It eats
the slow ones.*

—Mother Nature

Sometimes it appears nature may dabble in compassion. It
looks that way when elephants gather around their wounded fellow
or when dolphins buoy up their injured companion for air. Humans
dote on the love and affection they perceive in the maternal
behavior of all sorts of critters, especially cute fuzzy little
mammals. But if you watch long enough, you will see every
species abandon an animal which has become a bad investment
of the herd's limited resources. Humans love to idealize animal
behavior, but the only lesson to be learned is that nature honors
the system it has operated on for millions of years. Survival.

The proud difference between people and beasts, even those
cute fuzzy ones, is man's ability to manifest the appearance of
decency, compassion or reason. We know deep down that any
deviation from the survival standard is dangerous to us, but

doing so is part of what makes us what we are on the scale of evolution, as well as who we are culturally. The standard we Americans adopted after World War II—fair play—was a pretty good compromise between what we need to do and what we would like to do. Still our national standard was based on survival— equal opportunity for all but with the individual being responsible for making it or not. Then the "cheetahs" would weed out the unsuccessful scholars, athletes, businessmen, politicians, political movements, nations and humans. What survived would be a hardy group and a strong culture.

Before long though, the concept of all people being the same came into its own in America. All the prophets of this particular salvation must have been only children, because they seemed not to notice that in most families the brothers and sisters are different. They have varying talents, drives, tastes and a broad range of bad habits and failings. Even with slavish devotion to equal nurturing for all, siblings always turn out differently. One is rich and successful. Another is a dismal failure. Most families regret that some children are less gifted, but they realize there is little that can be done to change reality. There is never a guarantee of equal outcome.

If ever there is a guarantee of equal outcome, fair play goes out the window. Try attracting gamblers to a casino that guarantees equal outcome. Try getting grown men, even liberal Democrats, to sit around a television set watching a Super Bowl game with a guaranteed equal outcome. Most of us want a level playing field, not a sure deal, because if you cannot lose, neither can you win. My liberal compatriots and I professed that the poor, minorities and everyone else would turn out just like us if only they were treated fairly. We knew better. In our own families we had younger brothers who were smarter than we were and older sisters with the character to actually amount to something.

Why did we have such a fire in our bellies for everyone to turn out exactly the same? Actually we didn't. All we really wanted was for everyone to play by our rules. We practiced our mischief for a lot of reasons; partly for job security and especially for power. Since we were clearly—though certainly not admittedly—a whole lot smarter than the folks we kept claiming as our brothers and sisters, if they would all just play by our rules, then they would be happy to acknowledge us as their leaders. In the name of "equality"—but actually only to grab what power we could—we planted the seeds for the destruction of individual initiative. Under the banner of Sen. George McGovern, we handed control of the Democratic Party to radical leftists and their moneyed manipulators. As model Democrats, we traded fair play for guaranteed equal outcome.

Then we demanded the fast gazelles get behind the slow gazelles and push. Unfortunately, when the cheetahs came up from the rear, the best and the brightest gazelles were the ones that got eaten. Without any gratitude at all, the slow gazelles complained that the rest of us weren't pushing hard enough. And slowly, slowly, a few of us began to worry.

Our private fears of a national day of reckoning began to grow. But it was too late to come clean, so we came up with a scheme to keep anyone from mentioning it.

Things are how we say they are, not how they obviously are. If you mention that the liberal emperor is lying, you are a bigot. The most outlandish lie of the Clinton regime is calling spending an investment. Your house is an investment. Your lunch is not, especially when someone else eats it. Humpty Dumpty has become our national policy adviser.

Our cover-up has become the official national delusion— *Let's Pretend.*

CHAPTER 12

LET'S PRETEND

*You can't get there from here if you lie about where
here is.*

—The Author's Travel Agent

In 1632, Galileo declared that Copernicus had been right all along. The earth revolves around the sun. The next year, the Lords of the Roman Catholic Church decreed that a bonfire be held in Galileo's honor with him tied to the pole. He had directly challenged the official beliefs of the ruling elite of his day. That was during the tail end of the Dark Ages, of course.

We, however, live in an enlightened society, so we can ask any question.

Nonsense! There are at least 20 questions the mere asking of which will get you run out of town. Flip ahead to the last chapters of this book, Insensitivity Training and Tough Questions. You do not have to assert any of these tough questions as fact. Just raising the issues will get you in more trouble than you ever imagined.

In 1956, Dr. William B. Shockley won the Nobel Prize for inventing the transistor, the most important scientific breakthrough since the Industrial Revolution. He later declared not only that intellect was inherited but that blacks weren't doing very well on that score. The validity of Dr. Shockley's theory of inherited intellect remains in serious contention today. But try asking for a rational discussion of the issue at most universities and see how quickly you wind up at the bus station.

A generation ago, the suggestion that the black family was disintegrating earned Sen. Daniel Patrick Moynihan the lasting enmity of the liberal elite. Today, scholars are dealing with the devastating reality of that very crisis after 25 years of hiding out from it. Whether any particular theory is valid is not the issue. The intellectual freedom to discuss tough questions is. The lord high inquisitors of Galileo's time could show up at most of today's university censorship board meetings and be presumed to have tenure at the college of liberal arts.

Censorship is an especially ironic issue in liberal America because "The Free Speech Movement" was a huge part of the Nineteen Sixties. The U.S. government was telling us all some outrageous lies—about Vietnam and a lot of other situations. You can't solve a problem while pretending it doesn't exist. Some straight information about the status of the war in Vietnam would at least have allowed some rational discussion. But President

is supposedly sacred? Very simple. Some real diehards out there still don't want to admit that not only are we all different, but that it is okay to notice the differences.

We must be free to dislike each other for absolutely petty, chauvinist, bigoted reasons. This may not be the best face of America, but taking away our right to dislike one another for the basest of reasons would mean this would no longer be America. Even the East Germans came to detest their Communist dictators for making them smile at one another incessantly and call everyone comrade.

Ask any child. You only play *Let's Pretend* when you want to escape the real world. But now, *Let's Pretend* has become the officially enforced game of America. If we keep lying to ourselves about where we are, how are we ever going to wind up where we want to go? How are we ever going to resolve the issue of racism, for instance, if we can't tell the truth about why people feel the way they do, even if their feelings aren't noble?

What we all seem to lie about the most is that we are all different, every one of us.

CHAPTER 13

DIFFERENT

*The first thing the Azerbaijanis did with their free-
dom was to kill every Armenian they could get their
hands on. Freedom is truly marvelous.*
                                  —The Ten O'Clock News

We are all different from one another. Did I shock you? Of
course not. But we have spent too much time focusing on
differences among the races—while reassuring ourselves there
are absolutely none—when racial differences aren't even the
issue. The issue is the differences among our cultures—those
vital differences that define what groups of people stand for,
expect, dream about and will put up with. The differences that
actually matter are not about skin color. They are about tribes.

The first law of the tribe is to kill anyone who is different
from you. Back in the Stone Age, that tenet must have protected
the tribe from alien afflictions and dangerous ideas. Ethnic
cleansing is not humanity's noblest reflex, but it certainly is
among our most persistent.

Our time-honored American response to cultural minorities

has been to absorb them. America has always had plenty of space, so the Italians, Poles and whoever else arrived here could set up their own havens of familiarity. That gave newcomers the safety they needed to deal with the rest of American society while gradually becoming part of it themselves. As immigrants were assimilated, they weren't different anymore. If they weren't different, then we didn't need to kill them. That not only made life a lot simpler, it made us think we no longer had any minorities. As we assimilated, we all became part of the great American race.

The problem is the assimilative process has broken down both for poor blacks and for recent arrivals from Mexico and Central America, although not for the same reasons.

OLD-TIME NEW AMERICANS

Since the beginning, new arrivals in America have undergone a well-defined process. It started across the ocean with tales of the New World spread by word of mouth and through letters back home from family members who had already emigrated to America.

The prospect of a new life with boundless opportunities created a state of anticipation for new arrivals. Even if frightened, they were ready and eager for change. Proudly they began to consider themselves Americans. Even the ocean voyage to America was a stark break with the old culture. During the ocean passage, family members drilled each other on how to say "hello" and "thank you" in their new language. They also exchanged survival tips they learned from earlier voyagers. Ellis Island, especially, was a dramatic and vivid symbol of the break with their old life and the adoption of a whole new culture. While friends and family meeting the newcomers might well greet them in the mother tongue, the welcoming committee made it clear that learning the English language and the customs of America was the first step toward survival and success.

Upon arriving in the New World, the old-time immigrants usually wound up in a ghetto surrounded by their own kind. But the successful among these immigrants made getting out of that ghetto their priority. That process began with guaranteeing that their children would speak perfect English and master the customs of America. Many immigrant families forbade the mother tongue in their homes. They wanted to assure the speedy integration of their children into a country so full of promise and unimagined opportunity. Their children would go to college, often with the families settling for nothing less than the finest universities in the land.

The measure of the character of these immigrant parents was their endless sacrifice for their children. They sought to be like their new brothers and sisters—not to dwell upon the differences. Yet at the same time they treasured their roots and never forgot the rich and varied cultures they brought with them from the Old Country.

Those who could not or would not do this did not fare well.

SU CASA ES MI CASA

Today's illegal arrivals from Mexico and Central America go through an entirely different process that does not work.

Many of them do not consider their move to "Norte America" to be permanent. Nor do they see themselves as "new Americans," because in their hearts they remain Salvadorans, Mexicans or whatever. They take welfare money and public services from U.S. taxpayers while sending their earnings home. For them, there is no Ellis Island experience. There is no clear break with the past. The folklore passed on is not about honoring the culture of the new land. It is about how to beat the system. Social welfare agencies note that learning English is of no particular priority and the advisability of learning American customs has never crossed illegal immigrants' minds. Learning the language and the patterns of the new country has always been the key to immigrant success in America, but this exponentially-multiplying group has taken a course that will keep them poor, ultimately angry, and a constant social and economic problem for American taxpayers.

Even immigrants from the most remote Central American

mountainside village grew up with respect for the customs and laws of their birthplaces. By the very act of sneaking across the U.S. border, these people learn that we either have no laws or have no will to enforce them. We should not be surprised when they conclude that we have no culture either and, consequently, nothing of value for them to learn. The new illegal arrivals have not been required to play by the same rules as previous waves of immigrants were. We Americans have never respected laws that are snickered at and unenforced, so there is little reason for us to expect the illegals to respect them either. This lack of respect spills over to our other laws, too, and even more dangerously to our culture at large.

PLAYING BY THE RULES

Asking why most Asian immigrants to the U.S. soon thrive, with little public assistance, will get you hooted out of any gathering of high-minded liberals. Perhaps the reason is that their journey looks more like traditional emigration. They travel a long distance across a large body of water. They come here to stay. And a huge proportion of the Asian immigrants are shopkeepers, skilled laborers and professionals, not illiterate field hands with boundless reproductive ambitions.

The Asians are much more oriented toward cultural survival through adoption of their new country's language and rules of behavior, as evidenced by their cottage industry of teaching one another English and our customs. Is this because Asian languages and cultures that all Americans see as the same are, in fact, radically different from one another? Thus Asians coming here are adroit in multi-cultural situations. These Asian groups are certainly not homogeneous. They hold ancient hostilities that rival the Bosnians and Serbs. However, Asian adaptability does not reflect disrespect for their past. They can simply become multi-lingual and multi-cultural. Most Central Americans, however, remain fixated on their old ways.

Legal immigrants, of all nationalities, assimilate into the American culture far more successfully. First, they play the game by the rules. They enter the United States legally and continue to honor our laws. A person who learns and obeys the laws and customs of the land tends to do better in life than a lawbreaker. Also, legal residency is an investment in future U.S. citizenship. Legal immigrants have something to lose.

Illegal aliens, by breaking the first law they encounter, have chosen to be outlaws and can only hope to live on the fringes of the culture and the economy. We best serve our new arrivals by giving them a crash course in civics, starting at our borders. Strictly-enforced immigration policies socialize the newcomers, starting them on the road to being worthwhile neighbors.

Yet liberal policies encourage people to enter the country as criminals, to live as illiterate outlaws and to subsist on welfare. Why do bleeding hearts burden us with an endless supply of huddled masses? Because liberal Democrats see themselves as saviours, not as providers. Providing is our job, whether we like it or not.

A liberal is someone who shows up at your house one morning with a cute little homeless puppy. He wants the puppy to have a good home—yours. You agree, but the next day the liberal is back, with another puppy. And another. And another. But he never brings any puppy food and he passes a law against housebreaking puppies and giving them rabies shots. When you suggest getting his dog fixed, he calls you a barbarian and starts putting puppies in your backyard at night. Ask the governors of Texas, California and Florida how much it costs to provide for and clean up after an endless stream of puppies.

SEPARATE AND UNEQUAL

For entirely different reasons, blacks have remained a separate and unequal culture in America for centuries. For much of that time, profoundly stupid laws prohibited black assimilation.

The obvious difference between the blacks and the European immigrants was skin color. However, skin color is not the problem. Culture is. The real reason Italian immigrants were suspect was not that their names were different, that they might look vaguely different, or have a funny accent. They were mistrusted because their culture was foreign and thus threatening. They seemed like a different tribe that needed to be killed or held at bay for the benefit of "our tribe." American history indicates that the very pale-skinned Danes, Scotch-Irish and Eastern European immigrants were originally treated not much better than newly-freed black slaves. In the Nineteen Thirties, white refugees from the Oklahoma dustbowl were met at the state line by white Californians. The "Okies" were sometimes turned back by force, unwelcomed by countrymen who looked just like them.

Without ignoring the human suffering and dignity issues, the truly damaging long-term effect of black slavery and Scotch-Irish indentured servitude was that they made it harder for each group to integrate culturally into American society. That the American establishment figured out a number of ways to keep the cultural aspects of black slavery going long after the Emancipation Proclamation is more a result of this cultural alienation than it is of mere skin color. The best example of enforced cultural alienation was separate and by no means equal schools. Both a literal and figurative "no colored allowed" sign was hung across every doorway to equal opportunity in America.

THE OLD COUNTRY

From 1619 until the end of the War Between the States, black people in this country could be owned as slaves. Virtually all were here against their will. On the other hand, European immigrants to these shores came voluntarily and brought often fanciful recollections of their origins. They believed that their ancestors lived in castles and manor houses, or at least thatched-roof houses. But they were certain of one thing: the ancestors of African slaves lived in mud huts or worse. They were sure Africans hunted wild animals and didn't wear shoes. Whether they owned slaves or not, European Americans considered blacks to be savages. Consequently, they were persuaded that blacks were not capable of learning white, civilized ways. Skin color became a shorthand symbol for their own prejudices.

The problems that bedevil black progress in America flow from an incompletely-adopted American culture. With all of its defects, America's traditional culture has done the world's best job of providing its people with goods, services, security, happiness and a whole lot of other things. If you disagree, ask our recent immigrants exactly what they are doing here.

The end of cultural prejudice can best be accomplished by the removal of the black cultural outlooks that everyone knows don't work. These include the staggering illegitimate birth rate, runaway drug usage, resistance to standard American English and a tolerance of music that degrades and infuriates African-American women.

Having listened to someone else recite such a list of social ills, the normal human reaction would be to declare pride in one's culture and prepare to defend it to the death. Hold on a minute! If white America needs to be willing to let loose of its dysfunctional cultural baggage, so does everyone else. If we all had defended the status quo, blacks would still be sitting at the back of the bus.

Two very powerful distinctions, however, must be made when measuring black progress.

First, the ancestors of most blacks did not come to America voluntarily. In the holds of slave ships, no stories were told about the glories of a new country and the opportunities it held. A place you go in chains is going to look very different in your mind from a place that is the destination of your dreams. And even the most kindhearted slaveholder looked very much like the Dutch slaver who yanked terrified Africans from their homes. Yet peoples throughout history have recovered from massive tragedies. Institutionalizing the memory of slavery is in itself enslaving to generations of black Americans. It is also a career path for liberal demagogues.

Furthermore, how do you set a fair standard for judging black progress compared with the European immigrants? Even though blacks have been in America longer than recent immigrants, they are only now in a situation that is comparable to first- and second-generation Italians and Irish. The real opportunity for black self-improvement, for their children to go to college, to leave the ghetto, didn't genuinely exist until the Nineteen Sixties. The real issue is whether the blacks, who are in many ways like new Americans, use the opportunity—as did the Italians and Danes—to guarantee that their children master the culture, speak perfect English, go to college, learn the trades, embrace mainstream politics and all the other factors that turned the Irish and the Poles into unhyphenated Americans.

HELP

Slavery. Isolation. Inferior education. Denial of voting rights. Yet the worst impediment that blacks have had to contend with has been all the supposed help thrown in their way. Out of counter-productive communal guilt wrapped around actual hunger for power, we have obliterated Reverend King's dream of an America in which we would all be judged by the content of our character rather than the color of our skin. People who support a Black Miss America Contest—and there are several such endeavors— would not tolerate a White Miss America Contest. They also seem completely unaware that from 1991 to 1994, three of the four Miss America's have been black. Each was presumably chosen on the content of her character as well as her beauty. Those who resegregate America have us to the point where our government carefully makes note of our race to make certain that no one else is noting our race. Dr. King would be tormented by what we have done to his dream.

NO COMPRENDE

How would the German settlers have fared if the public schools of the day believed in bilingual education? If the entire system had not forced the Ukrainians and Serbians to become Americans or starve, where would they be? For that matter, where would any of us be?

If we need a chance to test our theory of bilingual education and racial favoritism, the Central American illegals will provide an immediate opportunity.

What they choose to do with their first generation in America will provide a lot of answers on the application of *Let's Pretend* to a huge group of people. If it results in the first generation of native-born Central American-Americans replicating the experience of the Italians, then within 20 years we will see their children becoming congressmen, business owners, educators, lawyers and on and on. If we do not, the results of the experiment will be obvious. Unfortunately, the outcome of the experiment will then make little difference. In our supposed generosity, we will have doomed another people to a life of separateness and privation.

CANNIBALS

It is very popular now to allocate millions of taxpayer dollars toward the preservation of this culture or that. But let's take a look at what we are preserving. Remember that cannibalism and witchcraft are cultural as all hell. Before we go discarding functional American cultural traits and adopting other cultural values of unknown or clearly bad effect, let's take a look at some we could do without.

Remember that the job of culture is to allow a group to survive, prosper and be happy. More than two-thirds of black babies born in this country are illegitimate. This is cultural suicide. So is the explosion of drug addiction in the black community. And the high unemployment rate is deadly.

The black political establishment knows that tolerance of the drug trade, fatherless children, disdain for proper English and an endless supply of tax-supported babies leads to certain cultural disaster. Yet the taxpayers, whatever their race, who grumble are castigated as bigots. This is the down and dirty version of the game of *Let's Pretend*.

Our differences are what make us valuable to one another. But when *Let's Pretend* turns America into warring camps, those very differences will become our downfall. If acknowledged and dealt with, our variety will make us immortal—the American Race. If we cannot talk honestly about lifestyles that undermine the American culture simply because they are more prevalent among some populations, our whole world will be about lying and its futile results, just like so-called "affirmative action."

CHAPTER 14

AFFIRMATIVE ACTION

Remember the first time you realized your grand-
father was letting you win at cards? Remember how
mad it made you? That's affirmative action.

—The Author

Making someone think he is winning when he is not may be perfectly acceptable and even admirable with small children. After all, it is only cards and they are only children. Like training wheels on a bicycle, this sort of make-believe builds confidence and skill. But lying to the kids about training wheels can lead to physical disaster, so we don't do it. We explain to them the difference between a real bike and a kiddie bike.

Treating minorities like small children is one of the nastiest aspects of liberal policy. Not only is that attitude demeaning, many minorities recognize it as an attempt to purchase their votes or to persuade them not to vote their own long-range interests. Most people who have made it the hard way feel this paternalism brands them as not having earned their success.

History is full of ambitious societies trying to declare things to be other than the way they really are. Remember Mao Tse Tung's Great Leap Forward. He would declare that on Tuesday morning everyone would be handsome, well-educated and have a full stomach. This worked okay until the Chinese people noticed that they looked and acted pretty much the same and their stomachs still growled.

There are some things that are extremely difficult to lie about effectively.

WEIRD SCIENCE

In 1897, the Indiana Legislature took an early lead in affirmative action. To make science and math easier on the school kids, the Hoosier lawmakers approved a bill that would have established that $Pi = 3.00$. Then a neighboring state attempted to legislate that water boiled at 200 degrees. A visiting math prof from Purdue University stumbled into the Indiana state house just in time to rescue the witless solons from this archetypal attempt to lie about the truth. We can assume the boiling-point fiasco ran out of steam when the distillery refused to function.

But the spirit of such stupidity lives on in Washington, D.C., with a Congress that really ought to know better.

Giving people jobs they are not trained for and putting them in classes for which they are not prepared would make even that old bunch of Indiana legislators blush. Fortunately, we seem to have enough sense not to make a person an airline pilot who cannot fly a plane. And brain surgeons should be able to locate the patient's head without help.

But we have not hesitated to promote the untrained into the social sciences and "soft professions" on the notion that it is their right to hold the job regardless of the consequences to innocent bystanders. Even Democrats don't want to hit the ground at 500 miles per hour with an affirmative action pilot in the cockpit. But they don't mind affirmative action when it is merely the future of our children that is at stake.

BEHIND IS BEHIND

The biggest wasteland of affirmative action is our public schools, where the problem comes from two angles—the teachers and the students.

For the students, affirmative action takes the form of social promotions based on the whimsical notion that a child is better off learning nothing while hanging out with his homeboys than learning something under conditions he might find distasteful. The price is a full generation of kids who not only can't read but who don't even know which hemisphere they live in. And what's a hemisphere, anyway? Would you want to hire these kids?

The basis for this doozy was a heavy dose of *Let's Pretend* that all kids are just as able as all the other kids when everyone, including the kids, knows better. It doesn't matter why some young people are behind—cultural deprivation, inadequate prenatal care or any other reason. Behind is behind. Behind will never get fixed by lying about it.

Besides, the solution to behind is simple. When students are behind we put them in classes concentrated on meeting their needs, then hammer on them until they can pull their weight in a regular class. That kind of training is real affirmative action that helps a kid actually become something, rather than declaring him to be something he is not. That approach applies to language, too. Any schoolchild who can't pick up pretty good English in one year needs to be in a class for slow learners, not in bilingual education.

On the teaching side, problems stem from the notion that it is better for a child to be taught little or nothing by a person of matching ethnicity or culture than to actually learn something from someone who is not politically correct.

The solution to this one is also simple. Choose teachers on the basis of their knowledge, dedication and competence, with no reference to any other factor—especially race. A student might truly love a teacher with a shared background, but mutual affection will be cold comfort when neither the teacher nor the student can locate Australia on a map without the aid of a picture of a kangaroo outlined in neon lights.

RIGHT TO TEACH

The other fallacy of affirmative action in the teaching profession is the notion that anyone has a right to teach. Teaching is not a right. It is a privilege that should be reserved for the finest people in our society. Teachers have a job that is fundamentally more important than law, medicine or any other discipline. These school kids are our future. They are our cultural savings account. It is amazing that we are willing to use them as foils to allow some inadequate teacher to pretend he or she is not a fool.

That is what *Let's Pretend* looks like when it's full grown. And it's not getting any better or smarter. Still, this is not the end of the world. There is hope. When we stopped being children we gave up the game of *Let's Pretend*. We can do it again. Try this:

Remember when you couldn't do something because you were too young, too small, too inexperienced or too weak? Remember how you worked and trained and studied and rose to the challenge? Now, remember how wonderful it felt when you finally made it on your own.

When what we are doing is clearly not working, the place to start is with something we know does work. For all our lives coaches have put new players on the junior varsity so they could grow and learn and become competent. When they went on to the varsity, no one needed to ask if they knew what to do. Army basic training has always taken a mixed bag of kids and turned them into uniform, competent troops, because there is no time in battle to ask a man how good a soldier he is. No one asks for a free ride. And no one gets one for long.

Simple pride keeps most of us from accepting anything we know we are not entitled to, especially in competitive situations.

WHITE BASKETBALL

We would stand in line to hoot and throw paper cups at any white, second-rate basketball player hired by the Lakers solely because he grew up in a deprived rich neighborhood that didn't have a basketball goal or anyone to play with. Check the annals of affirmative action and you'll find a lot sillier examples than that. More decisions ought to be made by people like coaches and drill sergeants who are committed to winning, not to being social engineers. Yet coaches and drill instructors have always had a special talent and compassion for bringing along the slow ones until they need no special privileges.

Scrap the label "affirmative action"—along with the whole misguided concept it describes. Replace it with the workplace and school equivalents of junior varsity and boot camp. If people are behind or "disadvantaged," give them as much free training as they will absorb. Once they no longer have to apologize for the kind of job they are doing, the whole outlook of our country will change. When you know you are good at something, training in self-esteem becomes as silly as it is ineffective. Those who refuse the training will at least have the dignity of having chosen their own doom.

LICENSE TO KILL

Minorities have been told that affirmative action is a benefit. It is not. Affirmative action is a drug used to keep minorities in Democrat Dependency Syndrome. At first they may not want to, but each minority individual must stand up and refuse to be treated like a small child, patronized by Democrat plantation bosses and doomed to a life of never quite catching up. The Democrat power merchants will have to be forced at near gunpoint to allow people to get the training they need. Liberal Democrats don't want minorities to discover they can play and win on a level field. A super-achieving conservative black will not work on the Democrats' plantation. A super-achieving conservative black is a Democrat manipulator's worst nightmare—a black Republican.

Only when we consign affirmative action to the dustbin of history will Americans finally view minorities as equals. And not one day sooner.

Lyndon B. Johnson and his boys were playing *Let's Pretend* with the American people. The Movement—in an uncharacteristic fit of higher purpose—swore that would never happen again.

But here we are again. It's now the Nineteen Nineties. And believe it or not, my free speech buddies from Berkeley are wearing the hoods and carrying the torches. The University of Michigan, among a host of other hotbeds of enlightenment, passed regulations limiting what could be said and what could be asked about a laundry list of folks—women, minorities, the disabled, homosexuals and so forth. One Michigan freshman who expressed an opinion that violated the official creed got booted out of school. This violation of the First Amendment was so outrageous and so offensive that the ACLU brought suit and a federal judge slapped the University silly. The University, determinedly hostile to the U.S. Constitution, busily set about trying to rewrite the regulation to make it stick. Having removed the First Amendment, the rest of the University's copy of the Constitution could probably be used as a doily in the chancellor's dining room.

Today, this kind of thought-police enforcement has become the rule rather than the exception in collegiate America.

How you feel about these issues is beside the point. But censorship eats the heart out of a democracy. Okay, so what is it that needs covering up today? What is so horrible that it cannot even be discussed in the halls of universities where the clash of ideas

Chapter 15

One Too Many. Two Too Many. Three Too Many.

The rich get richer and the poor have children.
—Overly-candid politician
who didn't get elected

We have all heard the saying that truth is the best defense. Apparently the poor politician who was silly enough to make that obviously true statement above thought so, too. He was publicly flogged in the newspapers until he agreed to take it back—as if taking it back made it any the less true.

You don't have to be a demographer or an economist to realize it costs a whole bunch more to feed, clothe, house, educate and raise a dozen kids than it does one or two. In fact, federal poverty-level income figures are adjusted for size of family. It costs more just to be poor if you've got a big family. Poor mothers are pretty good home economists. They have to be because there is never enough of everything to go around. They budget carefully to figure out how much they can afford of the various items their families need.

One of the biggest differences between middle-income families and poor ones is that middle-income couples tend to go into marriage with a firm idea of how many children they can afford to have. And usually they stick to their child budget. So why do people with the least time and money to spend on raising children seem to have the most children to spend it on?

FARM KIDS

Family size is largely a matter of tradition. But tradition can change in a modern society. Many Boomers' parents were farm kids raised in large families. Since farms were not subject to child labor laws, farm children had an economic value to the family from an early age. Farmers and the poor had always operated on the notion that they could make room for another mouth at the table.

In the city, however, children were luxuries, not economic benefits. Smart families down-sized accordingly. The inflationary spiral of the Nineteen Sixties sent mothers off to work and prices soaring. Both time and money for child-rearing were in short supply.

The bottomless stewpot may have existed when another mouth at the table simply meant picking an extra turnip to toss in the stew. But today is different—markedly different. An extra child means an extra pair of $100 tennis shoes, a few extra pairs of name brand jeans, extremely expensive school supplies and dozens of costs well known to every parent, rich or poor. An extra child means more than merely an extra plate at the table. Also, with most mothers working now, the huge time requirements of an extra child have to be met somehow—or often not met at all.

Credit clinics have sprung up in every city to help people learn to control their impulse buying—commitments made without regard for what the person can afford to spend on a limited income. Most Americans agree that irresponsible spending is a personal failing that costs us all in bankruptcy and bad debt losses. Planned Parenthood notwithstanding, our society has failed to take the same stand on people who take on an 18-year obligation to raise children whom they cannot afford and often don't seem to want. Some of this spawning comes from negligent sex, some of it is intentional, and some of it is simply mindless. But the consequences are the same. Just as we all pay for the bankruptcies of the spendthrift, every one of us pays to raise these ill-conceived children.

The large, close family that pulls and sacrifices together still turns out some of the finest people this country could ever want. The large, loose and ill-tended families whose children roam the streets in crime are worse than a dead loss to America. The conflict of American culture with the culture of illegal immigration is explosive. Many illegal immigrants have an overwhelming cultural history of extremely large families. That may have been economically sound in their agrarian native lands where conditions made children valuable to the family. In the U.S., however, it translates into producing economically valueless children with no regard for the consequences—to the children, to themselves and to their hapless American hosts who have to feed and put up with them.

SELF RESTRAINT

With the liberals' tendency to overglamorize other cultures, legions of puddingheads rise up at the slightest hint that a little self-restraint among our uninvited guests might be a nice way to say thank you for our hospitality. The unwillingness of large groups to adapt their behavior to different circumstances is a cultural time bomb. When we blindly maintain that kind of behavior is acceptable, it is just another round of *Let's Pretend*.

The suggestion that some habits are "cultural" has become a code phrase for excusing anti-social behavior. Cannibalism, however, is cultural and a strong binding force in many clans and sects in New Guinea and Africa. As a matter of policy, however, we do not tolerate the eating of our citizens. Even the most liberal would turn bigoted when their kids were invited to sleep over with the cannibal family next door. What exactly is the difference between eating kids and starving kids? The result of mindless overpopulation is an increase in the number of children who are undernourished and sociopathic. These are children who will spin the revolving door of our prisons and continue the cycle of unconsidered overpopulation. If we really would not tolerate a cultural group that put its kids in a pot and boiled them, why do we not only tolerate, but cultivate, a long-term result that is little different?

NOBODY'S CHILD

The net economic effect of overpopulation is pernicious. And it affects most those who do not get to vote on whether the taxpayers really need another child to raise. Furthermore, undereducated, undersocialized children create a disproportionate drain on our social services and prisons. And we must count the outrageous social and economic cost of the crimes that put them in prison.

In the long term, we risk living the same cycle that has made Mexico's problems so intractable; ungoverned overpopulation that will guarantee economic doom. A doom, incidentally, for which the U.S. taxpayer will likely pick up the tab. Mexico's economy might be able to expand fast enough to break even, but it will never be able to absorb its own maniacal runaway population growth. The United States has no guarantee of any different fate.

A PARABLE

A young man goes to his father and asks for $1,000 per month financial assistance because he and his family have fallen on hard times. The father indicates a willingness to help his loved ones as soon as the son has disposed of his Mercedes, taken a second job, and the wife has sought employment. The son then announces that besides the two children they already have, he and the wife are planning at least six more. The father's astonishment is met with the son's declaration that he and his wife have joined a new-thought philosophical society that advocates continual reproduction throughout the child-bearing years. The father says that he loves his two grandchildren dearly, but has no intention of financing a family that can't afford the children it already has and plans an endless procession that it will never be able to pay for. The son angrily states that the father is practicing philosophical oppression against him and his wife, depriving them of their free will. Whereupon the father announces that everyone should finance their own pet philosophies and throws the son out the door.

THE BOTTOM LINE

The right of anyone to repopulate the face of the Earth comes down to these questions:

1.   Does anyone have the right to have more children than he can feed, educate and raise into useful citizens?

2.   Should our society tax its workers to support other people's cultural taste for large families they cannot support?

3.   Is this kind of willful overpopulation and the suffering it creates substantially different from any other form of child abuse?

Respect for the Earth and this country starts with not over-populating it.

Self-respect begins with not expecting your neighbors to raise your kids.

CHAPTER 16
RESPECT

Before the Revolution no one liked me and I got no respect. Now I am a big labor official for the Sandinistas and I make people respect me. They respect me or else.

—Low-level Sandinista bureaucrat

This one is easy! What that man is receiving is deference, not respect. Deference is what you showed the bully in elementary school to keep from getting beat up any worse than was absolutely necessary. And deference is what the war-weary peasants of Nicaragua showed their Communist liberators, the Sandinistas.

But all bullies share a dilemma. A bully can't turn his back because, sooner or later, the oppressed of the schoolyard will kick the living hell out of him.

In adulthood, things don't change all that much. Now it's the boss, your in-laws or someone else you absolutely have to get along with and cannot avoid or abide. Ever notice the amount of time you spend daydreaming about the details of their utter humiliation at your hands? Ever so often, the news media report about someone who went over the edge and finally blew the boss's brains out. Gives you a funny feeling you'd rather not talk about, doesn't it?

Respect is absolutely unrelated to deference. Yet respect and deference wind up looking alike because that is the whole point of deference. Deference is supposed to fool the bully into believing that you respect him. Bullies are constitutionally incapable of telling the difference, which is probably just as well. Bullies come in all shapes, sizes and sexes, by the way.

You may not be able to recognize respect when you witness it, but you certainly know respect when you feel it for someone else. Think of the feeling you had at the best play or concert you ever went to. Think of how you feel when you listen to your favorite musician. What kinds of memories do you have about your favorite teacher or a first-class aunt or uncle? Think about your favorite athlete when he does the impossible. That is what respect is all about. Respect cannot be imposed upon you or created by "affirmative action."

WHAT WORKS

Blacks have long been well respected for their achievements in music, entertainment and sports. Curiously, we don't see much in the way of affirmative action in those fields of endeavor. You don't have to force the public to accept a person with talent, dedication, determination and skill; precisely the qualities that blacks have brought to those callings. There aren't enough black customers to catapult these people to stardom on their own, so apparently an awful lot of whites admire and respect those qualities, too. Anyone who was ever in a white sports bar when Michael Jordan was flying can only call the crowd adoring. That black guy was the hero of those white guys.

So why doesn't it work the same way in other undertakings where affirmative action has made even the most able of blacks suspect to their co-workers? Because in sports, entertainment and music, blacks worked and earned everything they achieved—no handouts. So what's the difference?

What Doesn't Work

My Movement buddies and I knew that the principles that made blacks great in music, entertainment and sports would work just as well in engineering, law or nursing. We also knew that hard work, apprenticeship, extra study and hours and years of sweat and practice were worthwhile values and were the only real keys to success. However, we had our political reasons for refusing to acknowledge that all people are different and have to find their own ways to success. So we helped trick an entire race of people into trading their pride and self-respect for what we persuaded them was their birthright, their entitlement: a shortcut. Rather than supporting, training and encouraging blacks to find their own way, we used them as guinea pigs in our social-engineering experiments. We used them as lab rats. We told them that their problems were imposed upon them exclusively by evil white men, and they could only be saved by high-minded white liberals like us. Many believed us, and by doing so they let us steal their power over their own destiny. We weren't even ashamed of what we were doing.

Today's Clintonistas are no more ashamed of what they are doing. They are still stealing black people's self-determination. With that kind of arrogance and the lousy results that have come out of affirmative action, a lot of blacks have justifiably begun to question whether American liberals really wish them well. The liberal agenda has had the effect in most fields that it would if, every time you went to the record shop to buy some classical or polka music, you were forced to also buy rap music and blues. At that moment, respect would turn to deference and deference would quickly become contempt—regardless of what you had originally thought of rap and blues.

JEWS AND JESUS

The most powerful engine of the liberal Democrat agenda is guilt—200 plus years of vicarious remorse. But if we accept the doctrine of collective racial guilt, where do we stop? We've got Germans and Jews, Jews and Jesus, Mexicans and the Alamo,

Serbs and Bosnians, and on and on. However, most sensible people don't buy the notion of collective guilt simply because it is one of the most corrosive, destructive emotions known to humanity. For sheer destructive force, guilt beats lust, greed and the other deadly sins all to hell. And we can never respect anyone who forces us to feel guilty.

What we Americans have to do now is find some way to back out of the damage we have done—through affirmative action and self-induced guilt—to how blacks and whites feel about one another. These two manipulative tricks have poisoned race relations. They have replaced mutual respect with an undercurrent of deference, anger and resentment that, if unchecked, will be the undoing of our society.

REPUTATIONS

Asian immigrants enjoy a reputation for hard work and academic achievement. Most people think Jews are good in business. Germans are good engineers. Japanese are expert technologists and thorough educators of their children.

Imagine the effect on black dignity if blacks were perceived as extremely dedicated, persistent at difficult jobs, constantly pursuing further education, dedicated to family, and quick to accept responsibility. If you are black, wouldn't you be gratified by this reputation? What black America needs is for the rest of us to quit trying to "help." Blacks don't need help to be respectable. They need the peddlers of Democrat Dependency Syndrome to quit rewarding unrespectable behavior through perverse incentives. It is still true that you get more of that which you reward and subsidize. Welfare begets illegitimacy. Affirmative action begets lower standards. Forgiveness of criminal behavior begets more crime.

Middle-class blacks and recent immigrants from Africa have proven that there is no racial component to having the right stuff. Any impediments today are cultural and imposed by an inflexible black establishment operating as agents of dysfunctionally liberal Democrats.

The ability to give and to seek individual respect is part of what makes us human. But we cannot live together in mutual respect unless we share a respect for our common culture.

CHAPTER 17

COMMON CULTURE

I'm having an awful lot of trouble getting the crafts-men to work together. Does anybody have any idea what the hell is going on here?
—Construction Foreman, Tower of Babel

If we were to be transferred to a job in France, the first thing most of us would do is locate an expert to teach us the language and customs. Whether the French language and customs were to our liking or demeaning, stimulating or a lot of trouble, would not be the issue. If you are going to work and succeed in France, there are some things you'd better learn. The French are terribly unconcerned about any outsider's complaints about their cultural heritage. If we want to get the job done in France, we have to play by the home field rules.

The same principle applies right here to blacks, Latino immigrants, poor whites, Asians and everyone else. First, learn the rules of the dominant culture. After you master the culture, you stand a better chance of making it nobler, fairer and more uplifting. However, if you don't learn how to play the game, you'll never get the chance to change the rules. Each of these minority communities must take responsibility for all of its members mastering the culture. Asian immigrants have done a remarkable job with their own family and community-based English language instruction and American cultural studies. For blacks and browns, their churches, social clubs, political groups and community welfare organizations already have the structure to get progress rolling. But what to teach?

HIP HOP

Like the hypothetical American going to France to work, you recruit experts from the dominant culture to educate your people about everything from manner of dress, customs, timeliness, work habits—each tiny detail you would need to get by in any culture. Teach standard American English. Black dialect may work just fine in some contexts, but when dealing with the dominant public at work, it is no more appropriate than heavily-accented Spanish or indecipherable Asian-English. Anyone who refuses to speak good English is no better off than someone whose speech impediment prevents them from doing so. Most people admire someone who speaks a second language or complex dialect. But an endowed professorship in hip hop might finally be enough to overload the sensibilities of even the most liberally-demented universities. If you object to public schools requiring mastery of standard American English, remember that the principal advantage mankind has over the animals is that we can adapt to changing situations, whether we like them or not.

ACTING WHITE

Learning standard English will have no effect at all until everyone in the black community stops ridiculing other blacks who "talk white" or "act white." For one thing, that attitude displays as much racial prejudice as the discrimination blacks complain about from whites. Your moral position is always improved if you are not busily doing exactly what you accuse the other guy of doing to you. The same applies to poor whites who are considered uppity by their neighbors when they attempt to improve themselves.

That denigrating attitude comes from an understandable human tendency to want to be considered okay just as we are. If we are told to change, we feel, then we must not be okay. Understandable though it may be, that is an anti-learning attitude. It will make any attempt by the blacks and poor whites to bring their children up to full speed, academically and culturally, impossible. We must stand by parents when they encourage their children to master mainstream American culture. Any fisherman can show you why he doesn't need a lid on his crab bucket. It is the crabs' instinct to pull an uppity crab making a break for it back into the pot.

THE OTHER UGLY AMERICANS

The illegal hordes arriving here from Latin America make no effort to learn even a few polite phrases in the host language. Is there any wonder why they are treated with hostility? They should think about the "ugly American" tourists who came to their countries and exhibited disrespect for the people and their culture.

Most of these illegals haven't bothered to learn enough English to make a difference in their lives. Furthermore, many have learned absolutely nothing about American culture, so they go right on living by rules that were appropriate in some small peasant village with no electricity or running water. Is it any wonder that tensions are building here in response to what are considered "Ugly Latin Americans"? You cannot ignore or ridicule a people's culture in their own land without ultimately paying a heavy and justifiable price. The growing realization of the true cost of social services for our uninvited guests will bring this issue to an explosive confrontation. Already, the move is on for Florida, Texas and California to get back at Uncle Sam for allowing the only foreign invasion America has ever suffered.

The United States—more than any other nation on Earth—is a truly multiracial society. If you take away our different races, there would be no America left. But let's not get that confused with the Tower of Babel Construction Company. When the people who share a country do not adhere to a single main culture and language, the result is chaos. Some things haven't changed that much since Biblical times.

Unfortunately, liberals are obsessed with anything not American. They hold our nation's traditional values in contempt. Why else do they fail to declare that multi-culturalism will not work? Has French separatism made Canada a stronger nation? If our culture really deserves the contempt in which liberal fascists hold it, why don't more people walk out of the United States than sneak into it?

What we forget is that the American culture is an amalgam. A Jewish man and his Irish wife go out for Mexican food, then on to an evening of blues music. This is part of the American culture of the American race. What we did was pick and choose from the best of what each arriving group of immigrants had to offer, discarding those creeds, customs and cuisines that wouldn't work well in America.

The problem is compounded when new arrivals elect to reject American culture, operating instead on an entirely separate system, all the while demanding that the rest of us pay their keep. They make no effort to meet us, their providers, halfway.

National pride aside, when a Russian airline pilot flies into an international airport anywhere in the world (except Russia), he has to ask in English for permission to land. Does that make English superior? Only if you want to land your plane. The international language of aviation could have been French, it could have been German or anything else—but it is not. The same holds true for our culture. Guatemalan peasantry could have been the dominant culture in America—but it is not. So if we don't want our society crashing into the side of a mountain, we had all better fly by the same chart.

OUR COUNTRY

That's it! That is all we have to do to keep the greatest country in history on its feet so the huddled masses will have a golden door to aim for. Is that too much to ask? If learning French is such an imposition that we refuse to do it, maybe we shouldn't move to France to take advantage of the richness of their society and the benefits of their enterprise. Okay, substitute the United States of America for France. If people are willing to give up homes, friends and family to come here, why do they refuse to learn the culture and language of the country that is hosting them? More pointedly, if this country is good enough to break into, doesn't it deserve their loyalty to its laws and customs?

Look around! Our culture is on the skids because liberals promote the idea that rights and privileges don't also carry duties and obligations. In a free market economy like ours, we all know that everything has a price tag—even if the price is just being a good citizen and adopting the American culture.

CHAPTER 18
PRICE TAGS

If you give a man something of value that he knows
he has not earned, you require him to hate you.
—Chinese Proverb

If you have a right, there is bound to be a responsibility that accompanies it. Everything of value has a price tag. At one time we spoke of the rights and responsibilities of citizenship. The idea of having a right not coupled with a duty would have been as strange in the 1950's as the notion of splitting an atom at the turn of the century. But then along came Lyndon Johnson, who came up with his Great Society and that singularly invidious bit of government theory—the Entitlement. An entitlement is a right stripped of any responsibility; money and privileges the government owes you regardless of what you have or haven't done. The best example of a right without any responsibility is the welfare entitlement.

The welfare entitlement is different from most other things we ask our government to do. Before you can draw a social security pension, you must pay into the system for a certain number of quarters and reach a ripe old age. To get veterans' benefits you must serve in uniform—honorably. But to receive welfare, all you have to do is agree not to hold down a job. During the Depression, welfare was designed compassionately to tide people over until they could get back on their own feet. The personal pride of most unemployed Americans compelled them to get off the dole as quickly as possible. Being on welfare carried a stigma. It was never intended to become a way of life. Yet we are now seeing three and four generations of career welfare mothers who diligently pass on the family trade.

FREE RADICALS

If a man from Mars examined our welfare system, he would conclude it was designed to give people just enough money to keep them from ever trying to advance themselves through work or education, thereby keeping them in a permanent state of vague servitude.

So what really is the deal with welfare? Non-career, short-term welfare recipients say they feel demeaned and belittled by having to take public assistance. Most are ashamed and hide their plight. The reason they are embarrassed lies in the very nature of an entitlement.

Because the entitlement is a right stripped of any balancing responsibility, it functions like a chemical free radical. A free radical is an unbalanced molecule with a mandate either to break apart violently or to lose its identity by becoming a component of something else. An example is ozone, an unstable form of oxygen that is corrosive and just loves to rust almost any metal it touches. Just like the rust on iron, the welfare entitlement is corrosive and freezes the ability to function of anyone who accepts it for very long.

Why then do liberal Democrats support this corrosion of the poor they supposedly care so much about? Once again, we should look at the manipulation of the disenfranchised for political power. Remember, when poor people gain some success and become homeowners, for example, they become a lot less tolerant of those liberal programs benefiting others at their expense. They turn into taxpaying middle-class Americans. As such, they are less likely to provide fuel for the Democrats who profit from discontent.

The Chinese put it well. You cannot give a man a substantial gift and expect to keep his friendship. There is something in every human being that distrusts a free ride. We either assume the giver is setting us up and the deal has a hook in it, or we judge the giver to be a fool. Neither is the basis for a friendship based on mutual trust and respect.

Our inborn distrust of a "free lunch" gives us the answer to the dilemma of the free radical of the entitlement. All we have to do is require every welfare recipient to make a contribution in exchange for the money he is taking from other Americans.

A Baptist missionary to an American Indian tribe told of hearing a knock on his door one Christmas eve. There stood an Indian woman who had walked ten miles in freezing snow to bring him a small gift. The missionary thanked her and dressed to take her home in his jeep. The woman refused the ride, explaining that her walk was part of the gift. That is the kind of spirit of respect for the value of individual effort that can make America great again.

Like the missionary who would not demean the gift of the Indian woman, we must foster the restoration of pride in those Americans who live the welfare lifestyle. From that pride will come the beginnings of employment, of self-sufficiency and of a positive contribution, instead of endless, hopeless Democrat Dependency Syndrome.

In England, university students were often required to perform services for their stipends or scholarships. Being smart was not enough. Scholarship students were required to spend hours at the library, copying by hand the great works of literature. The university did not need these handwritten transcriptions. The tasks were required so that the students on scholarship would never feel they were being given a dole they had not earned. That the students might have learned something in the reading and writing was a bonus.

BOOT STRAPS

Voltaire said "Work banishes those three great evils: boredom, vice and poverty."

We must require welfare recipients to contribute. Let the mothers take care of other children so other moms can walk the sidewalks of their neighborhoods helping the old and the sick. Other ways to "earn" welfare would be to pick up trash, to paint houses, to discourage delinquency while encouraging potential dropouts to hang in. Pulling yourself up by your own bootstraps is not merely a cliché, and it really does begin in the neighborhood where you live.

The infirm welfare recipients can call others on the phone to see if they are all right and to coordinate public services to the community. The elderly can use their special talents to make things to please children and tell stories of history and personal pride. Each and every one of them can care about each other. Traditionally, the poor have been considered compassionate. They can use that compassion to promote their own self-sufficiency. The notion that people can maintain their self-respect in perpetual slavery to the welfare cycle is another example of *Let's Pretend* at its most destructive.

POOR AND DOWNTRODDEN

A leader whose power and fame is based on his leadership of

the poor and downtrodden has one abiding need—to keep his followers poor, downtrodden and resentful. For when his followers are no longer poor and downtrodden, he is out of a job—often a rather cushy job. Consequently, powerful self-styled leaders will fight the notion of work-for-welfare pay, because if we are all pulling together in common culture there will be much less demand for the ringmasters of dissent and promoters of victimization. Call this the Reverend Effect, in honor of churchless ministers like Jesse Jackson and Al Sharpton.

Another prime ingredient for demagoguery is hostility. Keeping people dependent on welfare guarantees that they will feel threatened by the loss of their income and thus be hostile to any attempts to fix a badly-broken part of our social system. It also assures the contempt of those who feel they are being over-taxed to support an unjust system. However, as the recipients become free of welfare, there will be one less wedge issue keeping all of our people divided.

Just as the agony of drug detoxification carries within it the seed of personal freedom, so too, freedom from welfare will become its own reward. Tolerance for the current system of keeping people addicted to public money is the essence of Democrat Dependency Syndrome.

We, as a free people, should tolerate it no longer.

CHAPTER 19

TOLERANCE

*Tolerance is how far a mechanical part can deviate
from the norm before it screws up the entire machine.*
—Most Any Engineer

Before Henry Ford set up his Model T assembly line, he first established the notion of tolerance. Parts had to be both precise enough and forgiving enough so that any piston would fit any cylinder. For his system to work, Ford also established limits of tolerance—or standards. To be tolerated by a cylinder, a piston had to meet standards of size and fit. No square pegs in round holes. Before Ford developed his assembly-line method, automobiles had been virtually handmade. Every part had to be customized to fit its mate. Automobiles cost a fortune.

Society is a machine with an infinite number of parts. One of The Movement's big points was that there was room for everyone—even if they were bizarre. We called that tolerance, too. By that we meant that not just white upper-class males should be able to become doctors and lawyers. We meant that not only people of the right color should get to go to school, to drink at any public water fountain or to sit anywhere on the bus. That notion is one of the truly noble concepts advanced in the 20th Century. It ran into great resistance because it threatened the status quo. But the resistance was not logical. A machine that accepts the broadest possible range of parts is going to be stronger, more efficient and more flexible. The same is true of the machinery of society and its components parts, individual human beings. Henry Ford made tolerance and standards work in his factories.

But plenty of other car makers went broke trying to use the assembly line, largely because they couldn't master Ford's formula regarding standards. They couldn't live up to the limits of tolerance that made the parts actually fit together well enough to work. Every assembly line has a scrap heap for parts so bad they cannot be used.

In industry, tolerance requires the parts to conform so they will fit the machine. But the liberal dogma of the Democrats decrees that the machinery of society must be bent, warped, twisted and hammered so it will accept the human components, regardless of how willfully nonconforming they might be.

Liberal dilettantes don't understand how things fit. They see no limits to tolerance. Yet we tolerate neither the abuse of children nor a broad range of other crimes against property and people. So absolute tolerance isn't a survival tool in our society.

STANDARDS

The one thing liberal tolerance will not tolerate, however, is the setting of standards. Liberals have gone after the concept of standards with a meat ax. Their assault on standards started in the schools and then invaded the workplace. They imposed affirmative action notions that place more value on a person's right to hold a job than on the customer's right to get what he pays for: to be served by people who know and respect their jobs.

The assault on standards was the heartbeat of The Movement of the Nineteen Sixties. We were contemptuous of middle-class standards. We denounced the entire concept of standards. Yet we imposed our own standards on other people. And we demanded tolerance for all—except for anyone who disagreed with us.

We confiscated the mandate of the First Amendment as our own possession. We used the ideal of free speech to justify chanting obscenities against the Vietnam War. We called decent police officers pigs. We locked innocent people out of public buildings. And we looted the shops of Berkeley, California. All this we did under the banner of free speech.

Once we had won the power that we were demanding, we took off our masks. We demanded that students be expelled from universities for making statements offensive to our sensibilities. We demanded that the racially insensitive be barred from public office.

Once we were on top, our notion of tolerance changed. We adopted the same reprehensible tactics we had railed against earlier—because our cause was just. If you did not agree with us, we branded you a fascist. You had no right to speak.

THE DEVIL

We forgot the advice of Sir Thomas More in *A Man for All Seasons*: "If you deprive the Devil of the benefit of the law, what will you hide behind when he turns round on you?" We became what we hated and forgot that a liberal dictator is just as much the enemy of human liberty as a *fuhrer.*

Now, a generation later, the invoice for our Revolution is coming due.

We ordered free love and now pay the price for sexual plague and illegitimacy.

We ordered mind-altering drugs and now pay the price for a crack-driven underclass.

We ordered academic freedom and now face the price of a generation that cannot read or write.

We demanded the right to total freedom from authority, yet we laid the foundation for a liberal orthodoxy that stifles the most precious freedom, the right to disagree.

Yet even the sacred right to dissent has its price tag—the duty to get along with those with whom we disagree.

CHAPTER 20

GETTING ALONG

*Anyone who has ever lived in an army barracks knows
the importance of getting along. It's what keeps people
in tight quarters from killing one another.*

—A Soldier

Getting along is an element of survival and it has two parts.
Don't give offense. Don't take offense.

Liberal fascists are obsessed with preventing us from doing,
saying or even thinking anything that might offend a long list of
self-proclaimed victims. Liberal manipulators have made truth-
telling verboten. On campuses across America, a casual comment
that offends the liberal elite exposes a student to expulsion or
forced reeducation. The mandate of the Politically Correct is clear.
Don't give offense.

Yet the liberal cabal has no grasp of the second element of
getting along: take care not to take offense. Not taking offense is
tough because our country is awash in hypersensitivity groups.
They include environmentalists, pro-choicers, pro-lifers, the
religious right, atheists, flag-burners, flag-wavers and an endless

stream of ain't-it-awful platoons. Each group has brigades of pre-offended protesters whose rage lacks only an immediate target. Watch the evening news. You will know them by their whines and moans.

But what if their opponent gives in or their pet disaster falls through? Then you have a street full of wildly indignant people with no place to go. Sometimes they simply go off to create some nuisance on their own. But often they shop around for something else to be offended by. For example, in 1989, after the Galileo space probe took off successfully without covering everyone in Florida with plutonium dust, the protesters just climbed the fence of an entirely unrelated project down the road. These people are cause junkies—"causies"—who show up at protest after protest, often bemoaning unrelated issues. As we in the Nineteen Sixties well knew—protest is power and protest is fun. Protest is also a potent aphrodisiac.

THE VICARIOUSLY WOUNDED

An enormous amount of this country's misery flows from an excessive emphasis on the first part of the recipe for getting along, while ignoring the second. Not only do causies go to great lengths to take offense, they wallow in it, especially when the cause is glamorous. They become enraged when anyone dares to speak a disagreeable truth or to hold an opinion they don't endorse. They meet their enemies with legions of the vicariously wounded, poised to suffer great persecution on cue. Some causes do deserve moral outcry by decent people. But most causes are only over-hyped opportunities for someone to put his boot on the other guy's neck. Like a lot of things, the topic is power.

Here is an example everyone can relate to. All spouses have accumulated at least a hundred certifiably good reasons to strangle their mates barehanded. However, if they take such offense often, their marriage has a short future. Getting along with someone who is less than perfect is the foundation of most functional marriages. Likewise, as Americans we are pretty much stuck with one another, so a little bit of that kind of tolerance could make life a lot more bearable for the whole bunch of us.

POLITICAL PANTY RAIDS

Most street protests are no more high-minded than our Nineteen Sixties political panty raid of throwing the Dean out of his office. The way to deal with causies is a simple adjustment in the attitude of all those folks sitting at home watching the tube. Whenever some self-anointed political ringmaster brings in the clowns, switch to Julia Child or to Barney the purple dinosaur. As with most street circuses, when there is no crowd there is no show. When the audience leaves, TV news personalities won't be far behind. Where there are no TV cameras, there will be no street protest. Remove the TV cameras, and those movements would be forced to influence opinion through rational explanations of their positions, honorable debate and appeals to reason. Groups with worthwhile positions to sell will make the transition. The rest can watch *Donahue* or some other intellectual equivalent of mud wrestling.

The First Amendment right to blow off steam, to vent our indignation, is a safety valve for those of us who have a grievance against our government or even a complaint about the rest of us. The Politically Correct exercise their free speech by cursing their enemies as bigots, sexists and homophobes. They take offense, lavishly.

But just as moral indignation is an American tradition, so is civil behavior, especially as Lifeboat America fills up. Yet the Politically Correct howl gigantic curses at simple citizens who state a few unpleasant truths. They delight in offending other people, while damning words and ideas they cannot stand to hear. They demand to be treated with delicate consideration while they call us dirty names.

CHAPTER 21

DIRTY NAMES

Johnny called me a dirty name.
—Former third grader, current civil rights leader

Name-calling is always tough because it takes us right back to the third grade—a time when our fragile egos couldn't take much abuse. The names hurt. Why else would the bully have shouted them? We were too little to fight back, but our rage was enormous. For most of us, this was our first experience with being silenced by force in the face of injustice. Sooner or later, though, with the help of the age-old parental advice about "sticks and stones," name-calling usually faded away. When the bully couldn't get a reaction, his name-calling lost its appeal. Name-calling was only powerful when we lent it power. Once we figured that out, the whole deal got handled.

Having experienced the rage of powerlessness, we must never forget that in our country groups of people lived their entire lives in enforced silence. Blacks, American Indians and the different knew that speaking up could mean death. And that awareness led to a suppressed rage. That same rage is now building in the American middle class.

Today, we agree that enlightened, civilized Americans don't hurl racial epithets. But is it really the words themselves that are so offensive, or what is behind them? Use of the word "nigger" is hardly uncommon in most black communities. The motivation of the one who says nigger is what makes it a term of camaraderie or a word of hateful contempt. Members of most groups use words among themselves that are offensive when uttered by outsiders. In fact, "son of a bitch" can be fighting words or drinking words depending on who says it to whom and how. The spirit of the occasion is what determines the slant, not the words.

Once, a good friend in college used the phrase "work like a nigger" in the presence of some friends, including my black roommate. The room froze and hearts stopped. My roommate looked up and said "John, I'm really not all that hard-working." We all breathed again. Then he said "John, you are a lousy suitemate and you always steal my clean socks. But you and I are friends and that's a common expression where each of us come from." My roommate then made some derisive comment about John's intellect and parentage and we headed out for a beer. We were buddies and we all knew it. If that's the kind of trust and friendship we want to encourage between blacks and whites, why do we keep sabotaging the possibility? Guilt is involved, but power more so.

BLACK AND WHITE

I pity my liberal neighbors who are so tied up in knots over black nomenclature that they can't relax and enjoy having black friends. What kind of deal is that?

My black friends don't flinch if someone in the next booth says the word white. But the spectacle of a liberal friend gurgling an apology when we overheard a stranger at the next table say he didn't care for his sister's black boyfriend left all of us wondering if the guy had a Klansman in his family tree. The black guys present said it was a stupid apology for an inoffensive incident, and we voted not to accept it and proceeded with dinner. We decided it was the other guy's right to dislike his sister's boyfriend regardless of his color. Most of us didn't think much of our own sisters' boyfriends either.

FEELING GUILTY

Since most people know you can't have a friend if you persist in making him feel guilty, who is promoting all of this discomfort about language? In the Nineteen Sixties, we kept groups at odds with one another so we Movement types could be the brokers and collect the power. Who stands to benefit from the rest of us not getting together? There are a bunch of self-styled civil rights leaders out there who look like they are making a good living off the same deal we pulled in the Sixties.

Any good electrician can tell you that when there is difference and tension there will also be power. If blacks and whites work out their differences, an awful lot of power is going to drain from the hands of an awful lot of liberals—black and white. That goes for Teddy Kennedy as well as the *Let's Pretend* "Reverend" Al Sharpton.

Keeping the races at odds with one another is a scam. We cannot treat it seriously. If we do, our sense of justice ought to demand that we strive for some balance. If racial slurs by whites are to be unacceptable, then so must racial slurs by blacks. And that really kicks the anthill over when you get to the Nation of Islam's Louis Farrakhan and his goose-stepping buddies. As readily as most Jews forgave Jesse Jackson's bigoted and tasteless "hymies" remark, maybe a little forgiveness is in order all around. So let's call a halt to the dirty-name game and get to work on some problems that really deserve our attention. Only don't be surprised if some mighty powerful people show up on the wrong side of this issue.

How silly can it get? As silly as redrawing the map of Texas. The National Association for the Advancement of Colored People devised a plan, approved unanimously by the Texas Legislature in 1991, to remove the word "Negro" from all geographic names in Texas. They even erased El Rancho Negro, a Spanish name. This cheap trick against 400 years of Texas history would also have left both the ancient Romans and modern Spaniards with no word for the color black. Regardless of what these places were originally called, the ploy that "Negro" is a term of dishonor is an insult to millions of people who still call themselves Negro. And that from an organization with "colored people" in its name!

Either we don't have any important work left to do between our races, or someone is creating an issue for his own benefit.

DON'T CRY FOR ME OKLAHOMA

The overreaching silliness of the NAACP's Texas map scheme becomes even more clear when the map of the United States is redrawn. Wait until American Indians have repossessed the names Ohio, Lake Huron, and even Texas (from the Tejas Indians). We can also presume that Texas will be without White City, White Settlement, and Whiteface, as well as without Indian Creek, Indian Gap, and the counties of Black, Cherokee, and Comanche. A map of Oklahoma will be absolutely valueless as nothing will be named anything at all. If you are not embarrassed by all this bullshit, it's not too late to start.

This kind of nonsense compelled Yellowstone Park officials

to change the famous "Chinaman's Spring" to "Chinese Spring." Okay, so if Chinaman is taboo, now what do we call an Englishman, a Frenchman, a Scotsman, an Irishman or a Dutchman? Giving in to this sort of revisionism is nothing but appeasement and sooner or later will result in the ante being raised. Surely, if adding "man" to the end of the name of a country is a slap in the face of humanity, our friends from all of those countries will soon be taking to the streets to stop such blasphemy.

PROPRIETARY NAMES

The idea that any group owns the name of an entire people is first-order sophistry. There are powerful forces trying to keep us calling each other dirty names so we will never become friends. They are even willing to change the definition of what's a dirty word just so the decent and conscientious can't keep up with what's okay to say. While we are getting rid of name calling, we could benefit by a lot less frequent use of the words "racist," "sexist" and "homophobe."

A dirty name is a dirty name, even if the bully is a liberal elitist long removed from the playground. Most grown-up bullies don't use their fists. Dirty names are their weapon of choice.

I met my first bully in the schoolyard of a little country school. I was in the first grade; he was in the third and twice my size. My friends and I lived in terror of recess. The elementary school was in a poor area in the shadow of Houston. Classmates appeared and disappeared as their families drifted from town to town seeking work. One day a quiet, slight towheaded second-grader showed up on the playground. He kept to himself; the bully took no interest in him. The bully had focused his tyranny on me and my fellow first graders. One day the newcomer walked up to the bully and told him that he had no right to pick on children who were smaller than himself. The bully began to do the belly bump and said "Oh yeah! Who's going to make me stop?" The little blonde boy said "I am" and popped him on the nose. The bully saw his own blood and ran crying from the playground. My life was transformed. I had encountered my first hero.

A week later the hero was gone, his family on the move to the next construction job. I never knew his name. And I have never forgotten him.

The next year I met another bully. He was slow-witted and big. At recess every day he would chase me down and sit on me. He would pin my arms and rage would overwhelm me. One day in anger and desperation, I told the latest bully to leave me alone. He said "Who's going to make me?" I heard my own voice saying the words of my now-gone hero: "I am." Then I hit him. This bully, too, ran wailing in terror at the first sight of his own blood.

The next day he attached himself to me and proclaimed that he was my best friend.

What made my first hero, no more than eight years old, a real hero?

He rose up to meet the crisis of the moment. It was not his fight; the bully was not picking on him. He took a substantial risk; the bully could have turned on him. His actions changed the course of history, at least in our schoolyard for what seemed like a lifetime. Without a word to any of us, he set an example.

And he set a standard against which I still measure heroes.

CHAPTER 22

HEROES

Where have you gone, Joe DiMaggio?
—Simon & Garfunkel

In the beginning, God created man. Then man created heroes, because he needed them.

Heroes can be great people sanctified by their own heroic acts and sacrifices. The Bible tells the story of Esther, the beautiful Jewish woman taken as his queen by the Persian king Ahasuerus. Esther risked her life to prevent the massacre of her Hebrew people at the hands of the evil Haman.

Heroes can be ordinary people, elevated by courage and circumstances. Joan of Arc, a teenager, became a general and raised Charles VII to the throne of France. She dared death and paid for her risk by burning at the stake, accused of heresy against the God she served.

Heroes can be mythical, the origins of their legend lost in the shifting mists of time. Prometheus, whose love of humanity drove him to steal fire from the gods of Greece and to give it to the mortals. Enraged, Zeus unleashed the plague of evils of Pandora's box on the world and chained Prometheus to a mountain where an eagle tore at his vitals.

There may have been a real king named Arthur in Sixth-Century Wales. We can be sure his life bore little true resemblance to the Legend of Arthur and his manly but virtuous knights who spent their days seeking wrongs to right; whose quest for the Holy Grail would grant them immortality. Although King Arthur may have been real, the heroic tales of Camelot were mythical, both then and now.

ACID TEST FOR HEROISM

Whether human or mythic, each of these heroes met the acid test of the hero. Each rose up to meet a crisis. Each took on a challenge that was far beyond his duty and risked everything. Each led by magnificent example. For meeting the test, each received the reward of the hero—immortality.

Why has every society raised up heroes, real or imaginary? Just as the constant quest for survival is the first order of man and animal, society's prime directive is survival of the group. The tribe not only must have a constant supply of new members, the new members must play by the rules of the group. Some societies try to grow by conquest and subjugation. But the core of the group can only come from within; children raised from birth, immersed in the rules and values of the clan, the tribe, the nation.

Children learn by imitation. They are master mimics. We determine what our children will become by controlling what we give them to imitate. What role models do we offer them? As a society, whom do we hold up for them as heroes? From these hero imprints, we build in our children values, language, manner of dress, standards of behavior, hopes, dreams and prejudices.

Watch a little boy walking behind his father. He imitates his daddy's gait. He drawls, twangs or rolls his R's just like his father. Long before he understands the punchlines, he laughs at jokes when he hears his dad laugh. He even says the same words when he stubs his toe. Children are near-perfect "imitating machines."

Just as we must be careful what we wish for, we must be constantly on guard to determine the images to which our children will be drawn. For within the recesses of the human mind, nature places a mechanism that seeks out heroes and follows their example. Our children will be drawn to the heroes we give them, and will lean toward the values those heroes exemplify. From their heroes they learn survival skills.

The United States has a long history of raising up heroes, some real, some glamorized beyond recognition. Paul Revere was a Boston craftsman and shopkeeper. As a courier for the Sons of Liberty, he risked his life to warn the Massachusetts minutemen of impending British attack. At least that is how Longfellow tells the story to generations of American children. Harriet Tubman was a more certifiable hero. She risked her life daily as she helped more than 300 slaves reach freedom on the underground railroad.

In 1927, Charles Lindbergh became a hero to America and the world by flying his fragile plane from New York to Paris. He risked his life to be the first to fly the Atlantic alone, nonstop. Millions of little boys wanted to be just like Lucky Lindy; courageous, bold and adventuresome.

In 1955, a tired black woman refused to give up her seat to a white man on a bus in Montgomery, Alabama. Rosa Parks risked the wrath of society and became a hero to the American civil rights movement. She set an example not only for children, but for adults who found their own courage in her singular act of resolve.

Today, a once obscure German businessman is recognized as a hero. Oskar Schindler risked his fortune and his life to save the Jews on "Schindler's List."

We even make up heroes for our children to follow. Leonard Slye began his career as a singer in B-grade horse operas. As Roy Rogers, he made more than 100 movies. In every one of them, he would lay down his guitar, jump on his horse, Trigger, and risk his life to save the damsel from the bad guys. Whenever I was unsure how to behave, my grandmother would always tell me to "think about what Roy Rogers would do." Gary Cooper and John Wayne became the archetypes of the solid American male.

For the rewards that these movie heroes enjoyed, however, society exacted a price. They had to meet certain standards. At least in public, they had to behave as gentlemen. Even if he got really mad, John Wayne could not kick his horse.

Dwight D. Eisenhower, the hero of D-Day, was one of the last of the old-fashioned heroes. We saw him as brave, decent and wise. To a large extent, his personal life conformed to his status as hero. He understood the price tag of being a hero and played by the rules.

Yet even with a hero in the White House, a sinister cloud was winding its way through America. American POW's were being "brain washed" in Korea. Evil roiling mushroom clouds filled the movie newsreels. A TV series, I Led Three Lives, hinted of ordinary neighbors who were communist infiltrators; who had secret radio transmitters and hidden identities.

Even as children, we sensed something was wrong; things were not what they appeared to be. Ike, the great American father, was in the White House, but all was not right with the world. Every week, Ozzie and Harriet and Father Knows Best flickered across our tiny, black and white television sets; a picture of an ideal America.

LOUTS

At the same time, our officially made-up heroes changed character. Rebel Without a Cause took the lid off the dysfunctional American family; affluent but tormented parents and their alienated teenagers headed for mutual destruction. James Dean and Marlon Brando seethed with sex and violent rebellion. And a new generation of Americans was drawn to them. But Brando and Dean not only played louts on the screen; they were louts in their personal lives. Our heroes were exposed as unworthy. We loved them anyway. They energized a new generation not to turn into their parents, but to seek new leaders who promised a new order.

FIRST ARTIFICIAL HERO

America replaced President Eisenhower with a new role model. The first fabricated hero, John F. Kennedy. He was rich and handsome; young, sexy and energetic. We saw him as godlike. Yet it was a sham. He was a product of his own cleverness and his father's desire to have a Kennedy in the White House. An examination of the life of JFK reveals very little that is heroic. He was a womanizer with a taste for hanging out with mafiosi. But we needed a new hero; and he looked like one. In the continuing afterglow, we forget that he was elected by a tiny margin, probably manufactured in the Chicago political underworld of the Daley machine.

Kennedy's fortuitously-timed death saved him from probable defeat in the 1964 election and set the stage for his widow to spin the myth of Camelot reborn. What was a tragedy for the mortal man and a bewildered nation was a boon for weavers of a new tale of the once and future king.

GROUND ZERO, DAY ONE

On November 21, 1963, my father and I ate dinner in the Houston Coliseum and watched John F. Kennedy give his final speech. The next day, by pure chance, I wandered into a student meeting where a new constitution for student government was being debated. Looking grandly over it all was a young professor. Turtle neck sweater under his tweed jacket, pipe in hand, he guided the students forward. He was one of the new breed of college radicals; charming, erudite and quoting from Norman Mailer and the beatnik poets.

Walking to my next class, a friend from my old high school said, "Hey! Did you hear about them shooting Connally and Kennedy?" "No. How does it go?" I replied, assuming this would be some tasteless joke. Then it hit me. A bolt of lightning. I looked around. I saw the blank faces of students, bewildered professors. A secretary was standing in the hall weeping. Stunned, we slouched mindlessly toward the central plaza, drawn by some force. A current of whispering students.

America would never be the same. Neither would I.

Within days, the word "Camelot" came from the lips of the beautiful grieving widow. The legend began to take shape. The Kennedy myth drew together the Hollywood legend makers, the fawning pop media mavens and everyone in America looking for an easy way to avoid the real world.

The truth became not only relative, but inconsequential.

Let's Pretend was born.

Lyndon Baines Johnson took over the presidency and began to implement his Great Society, invoking the new universal talisman—"It is what President Kennedy would have wanted. We owe it to his memory." Challenging LBJ's proclamations became heresy to the memory of the fallen king. The entitlement and the modern welfare society sprang to life.

Like the primordial sea from which life is supposed to have sprung, the social sea began to boil. The social chemicals and compounds, already groping their way towards becoming more complex forms of societal amino acids, came to life. The lightning bolt of Kennedy's assassination transformed our society and gave breath to a thousand new life forms. One of these was The Movement.

In the strong sun of the memory of JFK, mutating daily into the myth of a reborn King Arthur, our view of heroes changed. Who could hope to compare to the ascended young president, never-aging, without sin. Who could pick up his fallen banner? His brother, Bobby? Martin Luther King, Jr.? Suddenly, they too were gone. The age of heroes had passed. So we changed the definition of heroism.

In 1967, the movie The Graduate made Dustin Hoffman a star. It also gave the Boomers a new role model—a confused, adulterous schmo. Then came Woody Allen who raised neurotic whining to a national pastime. But what they provided was not satisfying.

Somewhere in the Nineteen Sixties, we lost sight of what makes a person a hero. But the part of the brain that seeks heroes to imitate kept working. It went on automatic, searching and searching. Like a misguided lumberjack, the hero-seeking mechanism did not look for the best tree in the forest. It settled for the tallest. Instead of heroes, it found celebrities. We began to treat mere personalities as though they were heroes, according them the rewards that once had been reserved for the truly noble.

We pledged allegiance to the new heroes: Mick Jagger in lipstick, John Lennon standing naked with Yoko Ono, Jim Morrison and the Doors, exposing themselves on stage. Our reaction was, "You killed off our heroes. See how you like this bunch." Andy Warhol, the phosphorescent poster child of the Androgynous Strain, saw it for what it was. He said we would no longer have heroes. We would all just take turns at 15 minutes of fame.

Then Donahue and Geraldo Rivera showed up with brigades of daytime television pimps and their customers. They pandered to the exhibitionists seeking their share of Andy Warhol's "15 minutes of fame" and television audiences who had lost their ability to distinguish pictures of heroes from wanted posters. Our society replaced the requirement of celebrity with its bastard child, notoriety.

WHO IS NOT A HERO

What have we handed our kids in the way of heroes today? Take a look at the current crop—Michael Jackson, his monkey and slumber parties with little boys; the Trumps and their belatedly semi-legitimized spawn; Tom and Roseanne Arnold in their grab *de jour* for publicity at any price. And on and on.

Why do our children adopt values that we hate? Like a healthy cell invaded by a virus, our society has begun to replicate famous bottom-feeders rather than heroes.

If we would know who is a hero, we must first know who is not one. Who is not a hero? Athletes, movie stars, rock singers, big spenders, lottery winners and a Capitol full of politicians. What are they? They may be talented and successful. They may be rich, handsome and accomplished. But that does not make them heroes. It makes them stars.

How can we tell the difference?

Kennedy's fortuitously-timed death saved him from probable defeat in the 1964 election and set the stage for his widow to spin the myth of Camelot reborn. What was a tragedy for the mortal man and a bewildered nation was a boon for weavers of a new tale of the once and future king.

GROUND ZERO, DAY ONE

On November 21, 1963, my father and I ate dinner in the Houston Coliseum and watched John F. Kennedy give his final speech. The next day, by pure chance, I wandered into a student meeting where a new constitution for student government was being debated. Looking grandly over it all was a young professor. Turtle neck sweater under his tweed jacket, pipe in hand, he guided the students forward. He was one of the new breed of college radicals; charming, erudite and quoting from Norman Mailer and the beatnik poets.

Walking to my next class, a friend from my old high school said, "Hey! Did you hear about them shooting Connally and Kennedy?" "No. How does it go?" I replied, assuming this would be some tasteless joke. Then it hit me. A bolt of lightning. I looked around. I saw the blank faces of students, bewildered professors. A secretary was standing in the hall weeping. Stunned, we slouched mindlessly toward the central plaza, drawn by some force. A current of whispering students.

Has liberal America produced any heroes? Name one. Apply the Acid Test for Heroes. Then name one liberal hero, if you can. Why does no liberal meet the test of heroism? Because liberalism itself is not heroic. It does not seek that which is great and noble; it seeks that which is average. As the Democrats engineer an America of guaranteed equal outcome, they grasp for a world where there can be no losers. And where there can be no loser, there can be no winner, and thus no personal risk. Without personal risk, one can never be a hero. When liberals take a risk, it is always with someone else's life, land or money. And that, dear reader, is no Camelot.

HEROES LOST

What is the price tag to America of the loss of real heroes?

Decent Americans are empty from the sense of loss for heroes passed. We are filling up with unspoken grief, a grief that leads to anger. Heroism has been stolen by usurpers who prance, who preen, who pander, who shock, who mock, who flaunt, who flout our laws, and who exploit innocence and honor. This theft is feeding a growing rage roiling in the gut of middle-class America.

It is the rage of the decent.

It is the rage of the people who work hard, who pay their taxes, who support their children, who contribute more than they take back. People who limit their family size, who teach their children respect for the law, who know who their children are. People who teach their children the small virtues. People who produce goods and services and jobs for other Americans; people who make and do.

It is the rage of decent people who yearn for decent and inspirational heroes.

At the same time that the liberal elite has stolen our heroes and replaced them with circus freaks, they have tried to silence us. They have disavowed heroism, they refuse to lead, and they stifle honest protest about their malfeasance.

Their chosen tool to silence us is to call us dirty names. They have told us that if we object to what they have done to our country we are bigots, sexists, racists and homophobes. They have dragged us back to the third-grade schoolyard where the bully silenced us by force.

And our anger grows.

Rage

Rage without a safety valve is dangerous. In the American culture, free speech has been that safety valve. The right to blow off steam. Any good general knows that a healthy army bitches and complains. When the troops fall silent, the general worries, for they have either crumpled into depression or they are on the brink of revolt.

The silence of the decent American today does not signal contentment.

There can be no contentment in the hearts of the productive when the fruits of our labors are given away to buy peace with those who will only return to demand still more.

CHAPTER 23

APPEASEMENT

You cannot throw enough raw meat to a tiger to turn him into a vegetarian. He is not going to switch over to Wheaties.

—Neville Chamberlain's Veterinarian

When I generated the first draft of what has become this book, I asked a number of intelligent and thoughtful people from a wide range of backgrounds to read it over and give me their reactions. Their responses varied from absolute adoration—at least that's how I remember it—to serious questions about my lineage. Most astonishing, however, was how few had any idea who Neville Chamberlain was. When I looked over my list of volunteer readers, it finally came to me: most of my volunteers were a few years younger than I. Chamberlain was no more in their vocabulary than the members of Woodrow Wilson's cabinet are part of mine.

This brought to mind the number of times I have marveled at newspaper articles on John F. Kennedy and Martin Luther King, Jr., that go into detail about who they were, when they lived and how they fit into American history. Over dinner, I mused about all this pointless reportage to a journalist friend who reminded me that half of all today's newspaper readers weren't even alive when Kennedy and King were murdered. This comes as a shock to most of us who haven't yet admitted that it is not our parents who are middle-aged, but rather ourselves. Incidentally, Woodrow Wilson was the President of the United States elected in 1912 whose wife was suspected of actually running the government for quite a while after he suffered a stroke.

NEVILLE WHO

For the benefit of youthful readers and the members of my generation who slept through world history, a quick review is in order. Neville Chamberlain was a prime minister of England. In 1938, while Hitler was gearing up for war, Chamberlain flew to Munich to attempt to get Germany's territorial ambitions under control. The result was the Munich Pact, which handed over to Germany a valuable piece of Czechoslovakia's sovereign territory. Adolf Hitler assured Chamberlain that this concession would make him happy and that Germany had no further plans for expansion.

Prime Minister Chamberlain returned to England and proclaimed that he had secured "peace for our time." World War II broke out less than a year later. His opponents accused Chamberlain of appeasement and the prime minister left office with Europe in flames and himself in disgrace as the architect of a failed foreign policy. Chamberlain had not bothered to obtain the consent of Czechoslovakia before he handed over their land and people in his grand gesture. World history had been around a long time by then. Chamberlain should have remembered some of it.

So should we.

TYRANTS

Let's bring Chamberlain's delusion about appeasement down to a level that we all can appreciate. If you have ever eaten in a restaurant with a spoiled child at the next table, you know exactly how well appeasement works. With the screams and demands of their young tyrant flying past your head, the doting parents simply cannot think of enough ways to please him. If they ever did, the child would simply change his demands and start the process from scratch. Getting what he wants isn't the child's issue—his fondness for uproar and torment is. As the dyspeptic victim of spoiled-brat appeasement, you could suggest that a reasonable response to a disruptive child would be setting and enforcing stern but reasonable standards. Unfortunately, if those parents had the capacity for setting behavioral standards, the child wouldn't have been ruining your meal in the first place. It should not be too difficult to determine who taught the child he could get away with that kind of stuff.

DR. SPOCK

Kids like that have been raised—intentionally or not—according to the theories of Benjamin Spock, M.D., who wrote an enduringly-popular child-rearing book called *Baby and Child Care*. Spock is a big believer in permissiveness and a theory that places considerably more value on tolerance than on standards—even if it involves letting junior set the cat on fire so as not to "stifle his creativity." Interestingly, his disciples' notion of tolerance does not include the views of the people attempting to eat a quiet dinner at the next table who merely wish to be left in peace. Dr. Spock was also a vigorous opponent of the Vietnam War, considering it rude and uncivilized.

A large number of the children of Spock's parental followers are now in positions of authority in America, particularly in our educational institutions.

The Political Correctness movement in our universities, and its perverse intolerance for anyone who disagrees with its teachings and draconian enforcement techniques, is one of the best examples of what permissiveness looks like in full bloom. Under the guise of teaching our students to be tolerant and to embrace a more diverse society, the Politically Correct have developed an especially nasty track record of suppressing honest inquiry and dissent.

One of the biggest problems with liberal tolerance is that it always travels hand in hand with appeasement. To show how tolerant we are, we not only will put up with anything, we seem willing to do almost anything. Unfortunately, as with Chamberlain, doing so usually involves giving up something that belongs to someone else in pursuit of our own purposes, even if it is just the other fellow's peaceful dinner rather than a chunk of sovereign Czechoslovakia. The loss of our mealtime solitude, however, is trivial compared with the target sacrifice of the Politically Correct: our First Amendment right to speak our minds.

WORTHWHILE CAUSES

Most of us have pretty clear feelings on how to respond to the snotty child or the avaricious dictator. Where we get in trouble is with worthwhile causes, genuine or supposed. It could be the demise of racism or the removal of claimed barriers to advancement of the poor, women, homosexuals, the handicapped and a laundry list of the usual victim groups. Our sense of *noblesse oblige* always kicks in whenever we deal with groups like these. Why can't we bring ourselves to hold them to the same standards we apply to ourselves and most everyone else? Apparently we forget that steel is tempered by the application of heat and force, not by letting it do its own thing and excusing it from the laws of physics.

Mahatma Gandhi led the people of India to independence from the British Raj not by violence, but by the refusal to bow to a system he believed intolerable. He urged his people not to fight back with force, but to prove the rightness of their beliefs by bearing the penalty of their choice of conscience. His dignity in accepting abuse and imprisonment for his principles moved the opinion of the world and brought British colonial rule in India to its end. In his *Letter from Birmingham Jail,* Dr. Martin Luther King, Jr., stated wisely that "Unearned suffering is redemptive."

CIVIL DISOBEDIENCE

Most of us are familiar with Gandhi's and King's notion of civil disobedience, even if a lot of people cannot identify it by name.

In the 19th Century, Henry David Thoreau wrote an essay called *Civil Disobedience.* Thoreau advanced the idea that it is right to refuse to obey a law out of a belief that the law is morally wrong; that a people's obligation to their own conscience takes precedence over their obligation to their government. Thoreau did not believe that civil disobedience should be without pain, however. He also stated that people must be prepared to bear the penalties of conscience, including imprisonment. In fact, the stoic acceptance of its cost is the essence of civil disobedience. Thoreau was suspicious of "moral stands" that carried no price tag.

Whether we admit it or not, most of us believe that there is some point at which something is so offensive to our sensibilities that we would be willing to go to jail rather than comply. Presumably, our Gandhi-like dedication to purpose would rally the nation behind us and then our cause would become that of thinking people everywhere. But Gandhi neither expected nor received a gentle escort to a friendly police station where he would be courteously fingerprinted, fined a day's wages and sent upon his way. Gandhi was thrown in prison—a nasty, filthy prison. He paid a real price for his convictions.

In my generation, heavyweight boxing champion Muhammad Ali stands alone. At the peak of his career, he embraced the Muslim faith. When drafted into the U.S. Army, he claimed conscientious objector status, was tried for draft evasion and stripped of his world championship title. He accepted the penalty without complaint and with great dignity, even though his act of civil disobedience stripped him of his career.

THE CAUSE

Okay, cut to the scene of today's demonstration. Let's make it about nuclear power, abortion, animal rights or anything that suits you. The TV cameras roll as overworked cops lift the demonstrators from their supine postures and carry them lovingly to clean, well-lighted paddy wagons for immediate booking and release. The process will be repeated the next day. Later the demonstrators will congregate in a fit of self-congratulatory backslapping about how they have paid the price for "The Cause." Gandhi wouldn't want these people in the same cell with him. This isn't civil disobedience; it's street theater. The closest to heroes here are the cops who ought to be spending their time doing what we pay them to do.

By contrast, the early civil rights demonstrators in the U.S. were willing to and did pay a substantial price for their beliefs and actions. The defense of civil disobedience by King in his *Letter from Birmingham Jail* carries a lot of moral weight partly because he wrote the letter while actually sitting in the Birmingham jail, not in some yuppie fern bar. There is no comparison between the moral authority of those civil rights demonstrators and the vague socialites and superannuated hippies who always turn out more enthusiastically if there are a couple of movie stars sharing the trip to jail. So what do we do with these *Let's Pretend* zealots who try to wrap themselves in the cloak of the beaten and jailed freedom riders of Selma, Alabama?

PERRIER AND DESIGNER HANDCUFFS

Let's set some standards! The Perrier and designer handcuff treatment of present-day demonstrators is unfair to them. We have cheated them out of an opportunity actually to pay some significant price for their supposed beliefs and the free TV coverage they crave. We have callously deprived them of the time in jail that might give them the chance to think seriously about just how committed they really are to their particular cause. They really deserve better! How about fire hoses? Not injury-threatening blasts of high-pressure water, just enough to give them a decent story to tell their grandchildren. "My Guccis and Bill Blass outfit were completely ruined, but we brought the government to its knees."

PLAYING TO THE CAMERAS

As to those obstructing access to public buildings and thoroughfares, no one has the right to keep anyone else out of class or work just so they can play to the TV cameras. Substantial fines might help causies to focus more sharply on their strategies. They could consider the fines to be part of the price of organizing a rally where the TV exposure comes free. Besides, a little time in jail might enhance their credibility and make them morally more useful to their cause with less need to pretend they are the spiritual heirs of Gandhi and King.

Most Americans respect or at least tolerate other people's convictions, even when their respect and tolerance are not reciprocated. Still, the level of civility and rational discussion of serious issues is likely to increase markedly if we remember what tigers will and will not eat.

This is what appeasement looks like. If you can't readily

recall any good examples of appeasement, why not drop by your local middle school and get a look at what passes for education these days.

CHAPTER 24

WHAT PASSES FOR EDUCATION

Ignorance is the only slavery.

—Robert Green Ingersoll

Imagine a forest filled with trees ready for harvesting, tiny seedlings, and trees at every stage of growth. Foresters tend the forest until the trees have grown to a certain size. Then the lumberjacks fell them and send them off for processing.

At the lumber mill, the logs are divided into two piles. One will be sent through the rough-cut mill to make fence posts and railroad ties. The other pile will be run through the fine-cut mill to make fine-tolerance finish material.

The raw material for the rough-cut mill is treated roughly. The nicks and dents won't matter for fence posts and ties. They don't have to be exactly the same size—close enough is good enough. A little warping makes no difference, so curing is quick and dirty. Bits of bark can show. Who cares? The saw blades they use can be rusty. In fact, they can be the blades too dull to use in the fine-cut mill. The help can be poorly trained, since the blade settings are just approximate.

What do we have here? Two lumber mills, with identical conveyor belts, the same size saw motors, substantially identical equipment. The feed stock comes from the same forest. But the end results and the techniques used to achieve them are radically different.

Why? Because management has determined what the end product is going to be—rough wood products or finish cut products. The decision is based on management's analysis of the market—how much of each product does the market require.

Now, imagine a radical change in the market. Railroad ties are no longer needed. There is little demand for fence posts. Customers now want fine furniture and expensive veneer. What does management do? They retool the rough-cut mill. They put sharp new blades on the saws; they set the tolerances more closely. They patch the roof in the rough-cut mill to keep out the rain that will stain the fine-cut products. They tighten the training of the mill workers. They demand that the lumber be treated with more respect, because the scrap pile is more costly. They hire more carefully, and workers who don't want to meet the standards are shipped out.

Within a few cycles, the rough-cut mill will become a fine-cut mill. And the products coming out of both mills will be of good quality. The logs will have been put to their highest and best use, the market will get all the top-quality product it needs, the lumber company will profit, and the mill workers can share in the rewards of producing more profitable materials.

But suddenly the union boss arrives. He declares that the rough-cut workers are just as skilled as the fine-cut workers. He says retraining them is demeaning to their dignity. He says that requiring them to work to finer tolerances is intolerable. He says the rough-cut product is good enough and the market has no right to demand more veneer and fewer fence posts.

The mill superintendent assures the union boss that all workers who make the grade will be kept on and paid a comparable wage. The superintendent says rough-cut foremen will be trained by fine-cut foremen and brought up to standards.

The union boss demands that all workers, skilled and unskilled, be paid the same, immediately. He says if they try to retrain the workers he will shut the mill down.

The superintendent explains that the market demands a certain quality. If the mill doesn't meet the demand, no one will want their products. They will go broke and fail. Let us work together, he pleads.

The union boss scoffs and goes to the government, saying that the rough-cut workers are being treated as subhuman. The government enforces the union boss's demands and requires the superintendent to put unqualified workers to work at the fine-cut mill.

The skilled workers become frustrated; some quit. Anger sets in. The fine-cut mill begins to break down. And finally, both mills turn out only second-rate fence posts and warped railroad ties.

The market cries, we can't use fence posts or railroad ties to make expensive furniture. The government then declares that railroad ties are the same as the expensive cuts, and anyone who says to the contrary is a criminal.

The ultimate customers begin to complain and refuse to buy the furniture. They look to other manufacturers, even those from other countries. The market breaks down, the mill falls into disrepair, the best workers leave in despair, and the lowest common denominator prevails.

If the lumber were human it would weep at what has been done with its marvelous potential.

But the lumber is human. For the name of the lumber mill is American public education. And the name of the union boss is the National Education Association. The raw material is our first-grade children. The end product is now a generation of students who cannot perform. And the market is an America that can no longer compete.

The disaster of American education is not about racial differences. It is a result of the mishandling of the merger of two separate cultures, as the reason for their separateness diminished.

On May 17, 1954, the word came down that the Constitution outlawed two separate school systems, one white and one black. *Brown v. Board of Education* made law of the inexorable shift toward an integrated America, toward a sharing of one dominant culture as blacks and whites faced a coinciding future. Chief Justice Earl Warren stated simply that separating children in the schools solely on racial grounds "generates a feeling of inferiority as to their status in the community that may affect their hearts and minds in a way unlikely ever to be undone." Although speaking about schools, Justice Warren was talking about separateness.

CULTURES IN COLLISION

All over the nation, ordinary Americans were dumbstruck by the collision of two separate cultures and the powerful hand of government mandates. But the images of federal troops at Central High School in Little Rock notwithstanding, most citizens in most communities across the nation went along, with surprisingly little disruption. Students left their segregated high schools for summer recess and returned in 90 days to discover that half their fellow students were a different color. There were taunts and jibes, but there were also band and football. And youth is flexible.

But as the two races came together, the differences in their cultures came into sharp focus. White people, while accepting the inevitability of integration, saw aspects of black culture they simply would not accept.

WHITE FLIGHT

In 1968, Butch Martin (not his real name) graduated from a fully-integrated high school. Six years later, his little girl's elementary school had a complete faculty changeout. Every white teacher was reassigned and replaced with a black teacher. And Butch Martin accepted the inevitability of the changing times in which he lived. Months passed. One day as he played with his little girl, she ran inside their home. Momentarily she leaned out the back door and yelled, "Daddy! Where do my Coke be's?" In that moment, Butch Martin saw his daughter's future passing before his eyes. Within minutes, a hand-lettered For Sale sign was standing in Butch Martin's front yard. His abrupt decision was not a kneejerk racial rejection. It was about his child's cultural survival. He knew whatever life advantages he could give his daughter would be wiped out if the English she spoke were jive. That day, the Martin family became part of white flight.

As parents, white and black, hit the road in search of the best educations they could find for their children, left behind were the neediest children, with the least family resources. Into this gap of need came not caring educators, but power-seeking educrats. Seeing its control over middle-class America slipping away, the

National Education Association, the trade union of educational bureaucrats, pursued the fleeing families with fleets of school buses. What they pursued was not students to teach, but parents to tax and the power to administer billions of dollars of federal education money. Those who could afford it moved their children to private schools, more sensitive to parents' values.

WHO SHALL RULE

And that frames the great issue in American education today. The parents versus the National Education Association. Who shall rule the schools? Middle-class parents are becoming willing to say "Take my tax money but let me educate my children, either in a private school or even in my own home." The NEA says, in effect, we do not care if your children are educated at all so long as we retain our power.

How has the NEA seized such stunning power over public education? Simple. They filled a vacuum. As parents who demand the right to participate in the education of their children have taken their business and their money elsewhere, the NEA has become the client state of the federal government. The federal government, at the same time, has become the surrogate parent to the growing American underclass.

It is no coincidence that the NEA is one of the largest constituent groups at every Democratic National Convention.

The National Education Association now presides over, and is empowered by, a separate and unequal educational system that is larger and more pervasive than the one Chief Justice Earl Warren, speaking for a unanimous Supreme Court, thought they had consigned to the dustbin of history by the decision in *Brown v. Board of Education.*

CHAPTER 25

SGT. DRED, U.S. ARMY

*Some of you bastards are behind. But when I get
through with you, you'll never have to apologize for
the kind of soldier you are.*

—Sgt. John Dred, U.S. Army

Sergeant John Dred was the most frightening man I ever met—
225 pounds of genuine soldier, solid as a piano, tolerant of no
guff and midnight black with cold, flashing eyes. He shaved
with a Bowie knife that he honed on a rock and a strop. And did
five hundred push-ups just to show us how they were done. Most
terrifying—he was in charge of my Army basic training. This
was no *Sergeant Rock of the Marines* of comic book fame.
John Dred was a real live drill sergeant who had life-and-death
power over me.

For four hours we stood at attention as he told us what he
expected of us and what he would not tolerate from us. There
were plenty of examples of each. For variety he allowed us to do
countless pushups. He explained that he was going to teach us
how to survive in Vietnam even if it killed us. "Better now than

then," he said. We thought Sgt. Dred wasn't a mere human, and that was exactly how he wanted it. But his human side crept into his talk as he told us how he never wanted to have to explain to his "poor old mother" that one of his men didn't make it because the Sergeant gave him a break, was a little too easy, or bought his story about why something couldn't be done.

Then he said it. "Now you niggers probably think you have had a rough life, that you've never had a break. Gentlemen, I am the break you have been waiting for." I saw a few nervous smiles on the faces of my black bunkmates. Then he said the rest: "You niggers will get up an hour earlier and go to bed an hour later—because most of you are behind. When I get through with you, you may be no better a soldier than your white buddy, but you will never have to apologize to him for the kind of soldier you are." Perhaps he even showed a bit of racial favoritism when he told us he especially did not want to have to answer to his mother. What if she asked if a black soldier died because her son had been too easy on him? John Dred did exactly what he promised. He turned out a fine bunch of soldiers of every color and background.

By the time we finished basic, I still feared John Dred. He wouldn't have had it any other way. But I would have followed him anywhere. Sgt. Dred taught me one of the most vital lessons I ever learned. When someone is working from a disadvantage—

physical, intellectual, cultural—you do him no favor if you try to make it easy on him. You teach the needed skills, but you accept no excuse or substitute for his very best effort.

The all-too-popular notion today is that a person who is "behind" can be "helped" by being held to a lower standard or by being given an advantage or guarantee. Sgt. Dred would never buy such a notion—not today, not in the middle of the Vietnam War, nor at any other time. He knew each recruit was different, but his result had to be the same with each one. "In battle," he said, "there will be no time to ask anyone how good a soldier he is."

Sgt. Dred also told us about a childhood friend who suffered terribly from polio and was, consequently, "behind" as he used the word. Friends and neighbors wanted to pamper the "poor cripple." Fortunately, some wise, tough, loving parents had forced their child to work twice as hard, to suffer the pain of rigorous physical therapy, just to hope he'd come out even with his childhood friends. Were the parents cruel? Were they heartless? John Dred didn't think so.

Now is the time for our society to learn the lesson my drill sergeant taught us. A child raised in an illiterate home must work twice as hard. A woman competing in a traditionally and overwhelmingly male field has to give much more of herself. The short guy on the basketball team had better hustle harder.

Is it fair that the disadvantaged have to fight not only to get ahead but merely to catch up? Probably not, in the way we have come to use the word fair. But that is the way it is. Have our attempts at global fairness in public education resulted in better-educated students, in young people better equipped to survive in an unfair world? Take a look at the newspaper any day as we reap the results of a system trying to be blindly "fair" without regard to the differences in needs and capabilities that each student brings with him.

What is not fair is to deprive a student of the benefits of a viable education through some abstract concept of fairness.

If we want to be fair, let's stop tolerating the indignities that have been inflicted on our educational system by students who do not yet realize what school is for and educrats who see the education business solely as a source of power.

It takes a lot of courage to stand up to the liberal educrats who think the public school system is their private sandpile. One man who did was Joe Clark, the principal of Eastside High School in Paterson, New Jersey. He patrolled the halls, enforcing unswerving discipline; a baseball bat in hand to run off the outside drug dealers. He championed the right of students to learn in a haven of security and discipline. He fought to bring law and order out of lawlessness and chaos. The 1989 movie of his good fight, Lean On Me, is a must see.

America needs more Joe Clarks and John Dreds.

At the time, I didn't care much for John Dred's ideas of fairness. But if I ever find myself in a battle foxhole, I hope John Dred will be in it with me. Whether in personal crisis or professional challenge, John Dred has been in my "foxhole" and always will be—kicking my butt, pushing me beyond my notion of my own limits, and providing me with his unfailing example of leadership. Do we owe our kids any less?

SURVIVAL

Don't all parents want their kids to know how to survive? John Dred taught us how to survive—any time, any place. He didn't know the meaning of the word pretense. John Dred was the only real parent a lot of his men had ever had—the kind of parent who teaches his kids how to make it in the world. He was one of the two best teachers I ever had. He gave a bunch of us the education that public schools, college, church and community had missed altogether.

How do we get the spirit of John Dred to work its magic on America's kids? Kids who are emerging from a childhood without discipline, values, survival skills or very little real education. These kids have classmates who carry guns and sell dope in the halls, teachers who are beaten up and chased from the classroom. So what do we do now?

NATIONAL SERVICE

Try this—National Service! Not this do-gooder nonsense Bill Clinton is peddling. When each kid turns 18, finishes high school or drops out, he goes to camp for six months—a deadly-serious camp that opens with two months of John Dred's favorite style of basic training. Get up at four in the morning, make your bed, shine your shoes, and make calisthenics formation. If females are intent on living in a world of equal opportunity, they deserve the same training for equal responsibility. Young women will go to camp, too.

For the rest of their stint, the service youth can tend our forests, work in our hospitals, clean up highways, battle oil spills, work in the ghetto, save our wildlife and wetlands, and for the first time in most of their lives do something that actually means something. Kids say they want relevance? Well, this is it. In the camp, they will learn standard American English, how to plan and organize their time, how to budget their money, how men and women should work together, and how to treat people of all races and backgrounds as teammates. They will meet and learn to respect people from everywhere and in the process become Americans without hyphens. They will learn the discipline of the group; how one renegade hurts everyone. And how to inspire team spirit in the troublemaker who caused everybody's weekend pass to be canceled.

It is not a matter of the U.S. needing their services. It is a matter of everyone benefiting from the self-respect and sense of value that comes from contributing to society, directly and indirectly. This is the essence of the endangered American work ethic. To most kids, the richness of America is like found money. "Easy come, easy go!" is still a basic law of human nature.

Another law of human nature is that most people want to feel they can carry their fair share of the load. Listen to any veteran reminisce about his time in the service and the lessons learned there. This approach can lead us all back to a national standard of fair play and give every young man and woman a chance to say "I did my part. I earned my own share of America."

Some principles will be taught in the national service camps that will make each of our lives better—not just the kids'.

THE RULES

Imagine a world in which most people play according to these important cultural rules:

- A person's race isn't as important as his culture.
- A person's race isn't as important as his character.
- A person's race isn't really very important at all.
- Walk on the right side of the sidewalk.
- Don't spit your chewing gum in the water fountain.
- Some really nasty stuff can happen to you if you lie to

your friends and steal from them.
- The same is true with strangers.
- Don't pick fights with people you aren't sure you can whip.
- Don't pick fights with anybody else.
- Use the turn signals on your car.
- Never curse without good cause.
- Acting like a fool generally gets you treated like a fool.
- Most people aren't really interested in how unhappy you are.
- Wives are people.
- So are husbands.
- If you dress like a prostitute, someone may think you're one.
- Wave a thank-you when somebody lets you in when you're in traffic.
- Let somebody in when you're driving in traffic.
- Most people don't consider tattoos an art form.
- There are limits on what you ought to do to get money.
- Don't wear a silly haircut unless you are willing for other people to think you wear a silly haircut.
- Don't try to make anyone else feel guilty.
- Appearances matter. That's all most people will ever know about you.
- If it's not your car, don't peek in its windows.
- Most people don't care about how unfairly you've been treated.
- Don't chatter during a movie.

- Even if it's your right to do it, the other guy has the right not to like it.
- Don't believe what you read in the grocery store tabloids.
- Don't believe a lot of what you read in newspapers, either.
- Know that television news is a form of entertainment.
- Remember: all news media will outright lie to you from time to time.
- People like to be reassured.
- If you're so smart you don't need to go to school, how come you don't have any honest money?
- Don't throw trash in other people's yards.
- Don't laugh louder in public than you can explain to a total stranger.
- Just because your mother said it doesn't make it true.
- Just because your mother said it doesn't make it false.
- Pick up after yourself.
- Don't cut in line.
- Don't take handouts.
- Don't ask for handouts.
- Don't ridicule people who are dumber than you.
- Don't ridicule people who are smarter than you.
- Don't let your kids make other people miserable.
- If you put on airs, you may be considered shallow and a nuisance.

- Don't walk around with your shirt off unless a hundred people have signed an oath that you really look terrific.
- Don't walk around with your shirt off even if they have.
- Don't be surprised if people think the inside of your mind looks like the back seat of your car.
- Don't get drunker than you can explain to a cop in dark sunglasses.
- Not everybody loves your dog.
- Don't wait until April 15 to pay your taxes.
- Don't race the yellow light at the intersection.
- Don't treat rock stars as if they know anything else.
- Don't treat any other kinds of celebrities as if they know anything else.
- If you can't find a good reason for doing something, don't ever do it just as "a matter of principle."
- Don't be surprised when people treat you the way you treat them.
- Don't throw trash out the window of your car.
- If you like to call people dirty names, be patient when they call you dirty names.
- You can make somebody wrong, but you won't keep him for a friend.
- Don't steal your neighbor's Sunday newspaper.
- Don't steal anything else.

- If drugs really enhance your life, why is River Phoenix dead?
- Pay attention when the light turns green.
- If you hear a secret, don't repeat it to someone like you. He may not be any better at keeping secrets than you are.
- Don't assume everybody else loves your taste in music.
- Don't drive when you've been drinking.
- If you give your kids silly names, don't be surprised if they get treated as if they've got silly names.
- If it's OK for you to steal from a guy who is richer than you, remember there is somebody out there poorer than you.
- "Huh!" is no answer to any question.
- Wait for the passengers to get off the elevator before you get on.
- Hard work and honesty are at least as good as brilliance— usually better.
- Most people don't want to hear how much money you think you've got.
- Don't have solid black windows in your car unless you like to talk to cops.
- You can only take drugs for a certain length of time.
- You probably can't quit them when you run out of money.
- You can quit after they kill you.
- *The Ugly Duckling* story is still true.
- If you don't like to read, find some simple way

to make a modest living.

- Try not to prove to your kids you're not their hero.
- Getting laid isn't the same as being loved.
- You really aren't going to be the next Michael Jordan.
- Your boss signs your paycheck.
- Stealing from an insurance company is stealing from people just like you.
- If you must warm up your car at 5 o'clock in the morning, get your muffler fixed.
- The stuff in hotels was not put there for you to steal.
- A black leather vest and no shirt is appropriate dress for a costume party. Not much else.
- Beating up your child will likely make him want to beat up his child. So, that's your own little grandchild you are beating up.
- Better to be moving in some direction than none at all.
- Self-esteem is no substitute for self-discipline.
- Just because your buddy believes something doesn't make it true.
- Your imagination is the most powerful thing you own.
- Don't be surprised if you wind up where you're headed.

COMMON CULTURE

That is a whimsical-sounding list of some of the things that should make up part of our common culture. They are principles you already know, because you learned them in our schools of long ago, at church, from your family, from the neighbors and in the military. Remember, you learned how to survive in little pieces like this, not as part of some grand conceptual scheme.

Bad news! There is an entire generation loose on the streets that is not acquainted with these simple rules of survival. And there's a whole school system full of reinforcements. Give them one more generation, then see if you want to walk down some dark street.

When I was presiding judge of a small city, I was berated by a few high-minded citizens for suggesting that some of our youthful thugs should at least consider a brief career in the military. Fading the political heat was worth it every time a ramrod-straight Marine corporal, airman, PFC or seaman recruit came by to see me to say thanks. They knew my theory had paid off and they wanted to let me share their victory. My raw material might have been penitentiary bait, but the end product was first-class citizens and neighbors.

Do you have any idea who is teaching these useful things to our kids? If you're not, then no one is. No, things will not get better if we keep on pretending our schools aren't pumping out an awful lot of little villains—who are only going to get more adept at their villainy.

Even the good kids could use a little attention to their social skills. I guarantee, a lot of kids aren't going to like the sound of all this. Maybe that's another good reason why we only let grown-ups vote. A brief stint in service camp, away from designer tennis shoes and mind-numbing stereo, won't scar them for life. And they would come out of their training with a much better idea of what they want to be, what's significant in the world, and, most important, who they are and what they might become. They would possess the greatest gift we can give them—the rules of survival.

None of this is going to happen by accident. Either we do it or it's not going to get done. If you have had enough of *Let's Pretend,* real national service is a good place to start. If we turn our schools on their ear, we can do something about the little kids. But the only shot we have at the adolescents is mandatory National Service.

Maybe a lot of parents will be able to have higher hopes for the future than that their kids won't kill them in their sleep. Then we can get rid of *Let's Pretend* as the ruling philosophy of our nation.

The typical drill sergeant has a pretty good bullshit detector. Nonsense doesn't survive very long in basic training.

And people with a better Nonsense Test make smarter, better citizens.

CHAPTER 26

NONSENSE

*If things don't seem to make sense, someone you can't
see is probably getting something out of the deal.*

—The Author

One of the major failings of Americans is an unshakable belief
that things are exactly as they appear to be and that everything
makes sense (tempered by the occasional Oliver Stone-inspired
fit of paranoia). This is a charming characteristic, but it results in
Americans being rather easy to fool. If we are ever going to see
the end of *Let's Pretend,* we all have to develop a much better
nonsense detector. Here's a good test.

If the connection between the facts offered and the conclusion
reached in the newspaper or on the TV news reminds you of the
connection between the facts and the conclusion in *The National
Tabloid,* nonsense has probably entered the picture. Even if we
enjoy reading about it, most of us actually know Elizabeth Taylor
is not pregnant by Elvis Presley—or by anybody else. That is

obvious fiction, but part of the fun of it all is pretending it might be true.

However, when you read in the mainstream press that our government should spend billions to combat global warming or on any number of other horrendous undertakings—even when scientists cannot agree on the subject—that is worse than playful fiction. Your alarm bells should go off. That is not to say global warming may not be one of the greatest crises we will ever face; only that the facts so far just don't support all the trendy panic about it. Likewise about a lot of other fad disasters.

Whenever a pronouncement fails that nonsense test, read the article or watch the news again and see if you can figure out who stands to gain what when the story is believed. Most of us have no trouble at all being a bit skeptical when the president of R. J. Reynolds Tobacco Company tells a congressional committee that cigarettes are no more addictive than Twinkies.

THOSE LOVABLE COMMUNISTS

For a tougher case, all the news media told us Daniel Ortega would be resoundingly elected president of Nicaragua. That was obviously not the result. Violeta Chamorro won. The news media should have publicly apologized to the nation for their incompetent predicting, especially when they presented it as God's own truth. Okay, so where's the payoff on that one?

I doubt that any particular newscaster got a bonus for parroting that malarkey to a gullible nation. No, their payoff was the admiration of their friends, who harbored personal political affinity for the Sandinistas. You don't get invited back to a lot of New York media-type parties if you don't at least pay lip service to the evil the United States has done to the noble Communists in Central America.

The New York liberal media elite ignore the fact that one of Ortega's first moves after seizing power was to shut out all other factions and close down the free press. This is a curious oversight for the American media, which wouldn't even exist without our Constitution's guarantees of free press and speech.

That raises a serious question. It is the inalienable right of any news person to hold whatever views he wishes in private. But since TV talking heads make an outlandish living telling the American people to trust them, shouldn't they at least be the simple reporters they claim to be?

The media are full of editorial opinion, but theoretically it is supposed to appear on the editorial page. Is there some standard of honesty suggesting that news people shouldn't pass off their pet theories and projects as the truth? For a comparison, what if a doctor told his women patients that an abortion would kill them? What would happen when the pro-choice forces found out he was lying to his patients to enforce his own religious scruples?

News people call themselves professionals. But most professionals, like lawyers and accountants, are required to disqualify themselves from cases where their own personal views would interfere with representing their clients' interests. Well, we readers and viewers and listeners are the news people's clients. We need to ask them a few tough questions when they appear to be representing only one side of the news instead of all the news. Remember, more people have sold out for the comradeship of their friends than have ever sold out for money.

RED FLAGS

When a news item that was reported as absolutely true proves to be absolutely false, your red flag should go up—especially when no explanation is forthcoming. Likewise when the results are squishy and no one seems to want to talk about them. The public is at the mercy of the media as to the authoritative studies they use to support their positions. But we need to be skeptical about the opinions of the Asst. Professor of What's Happening Now at Leftward College or any liberal think tank in Washington, D.C. Lots of studies are merely the product of someone with a theory looking for ways to peddle it. If he is a successful peddler, he gets a big grant.

For example, the studies supporting the seminal desegregation case called *Brown v. Board of Education* were largely disavowed later by their author. He explained that he was merely proposing possibilities and theories, not universal truth. When these fundamental studies do fall through, we seldom hear anything about it from the people who used them to advance their cause.

The second part of your Nonsense Test involves the beneficiary. A TV preacher saying "trust me and send me money" is obvious. A lot of the other nonsense merchants aren't. When tracking down financial misdeeds, fraud examiners often go to marriage license records. When you find out who is married to whose sister, the mysteries of a transaction often fall right into focus. In ideological fraud, you have to search for the philosophic brother-in-law, although his identity may be shrouded in mystery. In the movie Batman, the Batman's dark and mysterious behavior makes a lot more sense after you discover that his parents were killed by a street hoodlum who became The Joker.

To apply the "find who benefits" test, anything favorable CBS news anchor Connie Chung has to report about sleazy tabloid television needs a careful look. Connie is, after all, married to Maury Povich, whose show has raised sleazy tabloidism to a new plateau.

DEEPLY HELD STRANGE BELIEFS

An awful lot of nonsense is the byproduct of people trying to sell us something for their own benefit. These folks are pretty easy to understand, for who among us has not told at least one transparent lie to get something we wanted? The purveyors of the leftist *Let's Pretend* movement always fall into this category. The really dangerous ones are those with "deeply-held strange beliefs." Eric Hoffer noted that people are far more likely to be willing to die for a belief system if it is truly implausible.

There are two kinds of *Let's Pretend* adherents: the sincere *true believers*, and those who have no idea what is going on but who have adopted the liberal litany for superficial reasons. Who knows which of these groups does the most damage? The sincere will do whatever it takes to reach their goal because they believe it is "just." The shallow have no idea what to do, and so are likely to do almost anything. The leaders don't care so long as their power game keeps playing.

The most outlandish deeply-held strange belief I ever encountered belonged to a young Hispanic soldier who could not speak English. He had just returned from Vietnam. He was in my court for doing 80 in a school zone, hitting the crossing guard, running over two stop signs and the town's only traffic light. The sheriff had to shoot the soldier's tires out. My courtroom was the speeder's next stop in the system.

His girlfriend, who spoke a bit of English, told me, "Oh Judge, I thank the blessed Virgin that his 30 days are not up." That was my first clue that a deeply-held strange belief was in operation.

She went on, "You know, when a man comes back from Vietnam he is not responsible for anything he does for the first 30 days."

Now the best I can figure, some sergeant had told the boys returning home from Southeast Asia duty to be mindful that they had been under a lot of pressure and probably wouldn't be themselves for the first month. They might not be very responsible. The young soldier figured out the rest on his own. So did I, so I suggested he be put in jail for the remainder of his 30 days because I did not know exactly how deeply held this particular strange belief of his still was. How an American soldier could survive in combat speaking no English is a separate mystery.

There are endless social notions the liberal elite have foisted off on the nation that make no more sense than the soldier's magic 30 days. Here are a few as filtered through—

THE NONSENSE TEST

1. *NONSENSE: BILINGUAL EDUCATION.* American educators profess to be mainstreaming disabled students so they won't remain dependent on special assistance or suffer lifelong isolation. So what are we doing with bilingual education? Any kid who can't pick up enough English to make it in school during one year of concentrated language training needs special education, not bilingual education.

NONSENSE BENEFICIARY. A huge bureaucracy has grown up

around bilingual teaching. Some folks are getting paid a lot in dollars and power to run it. Teachers who picked up barrio Spanish growing up enjoy bonuses as "bilingual" teachers, without regard to their teaching skills or English language capabilities. As a result, a lot of students are being denied adequate English language instruction. This will prolong their dependency on Latino political demagogues. Language deficiencies and cultural alienation guarantee the continuation of conflict. Out of conflict comes power.

2. *NONSENSE: THE POOR AND DOWNTRODDEN.* Discrimination is a word that describes the ability to discern this from that. In fact, traditionally it was considered a high compliment to be called a person of discriminating taste. So how did "discrimination" wind up being a dirty word? Interestingly, Jesse Jackson, a man who uses the word a lot, regularly engages in discrimination. He discriminates in favor of having a hamburger and discriminates against having a hot dog. He discriminates in favor of whatever he actually does and discriminates against whatever he doesn't do, just like the rest of us.

When you see chanting crowds condemning discrimination, what they probably mean to complain about is unfair discrimination or maybe unlawful discrimination. However, since a lot of these folks fall into the category of people who only memorized their philosophy, they think being treated differently for any reason—even a valid and lawful one—is evil discrimination. Since most of us don't complain when discrimination works in our favor, that reduces the members of the offended group to maintaining they have been grievously injured merely because something didn't turn out the way they wanted it to.

NONSENSE BENEFICIARY. Remember, leaders need somebody to lead. If your deal is leading the downtrodden, you need a whole bunch of downtrodden or you are out of the "I am your leader" business. One of the best ways to keep a gaggle of followers down-trodden is to keep them uninformed and obnoxious about it. If you can do that, the system will do a pretty good job of keeping them poor and angry. Then you, the leader, get to be a leader for another day and end up with a bigger if not better following. Who wins on that deal? Probably not the poor and downtrodden.

Occasionally, a refreshing if unintentional bit of honesty creeps in. During the panic over the spraying of the chemical Alar on apples, movie star Meryl Streep announced herself to be the spokesperson for the uninformed. Most causie leaders are not as candid as the hapless actress was about her bogus issue.

3. *NONSENSE: RACIAL JUSTICE.* A Mafia boss is indicted for jury tampering because he threatened to rough up a couple of jurors and their families if he were to be convicted. In the same city on the same day, a different jury hears the case of an accused police officer. The leaders of a race mob threaten to riot if the policeman is not convicted.

The cop is convicted. The jurors admit they felt pressured to find him guilty. Yet the leaders of the racial mob are never indicted. What's the difference between jury tampering and jury intimidating?

NONSENSE BENEFICIARY. Persuading people that mob violence is the way to do things makes it that much harder for people to function within a culture that condemns mob violence. In our country, rioting is not a survival skill. The integrity of our justice system goes out the window when mob threats influence the outcome of trials. The unintended consequence is the alienation of potential well-wishers. The beneficiary is the leader of the mob who has gained another example of how other people just don't like his folks and wish them ill. Out of alienation, even when contrived, comes power. The tactic is called "driving a wedge." You may also recognize the tactic as divide and conquer.

4. *NONSENSE: THE MILITARY.* Liberals don't have a complete lock on contriving facts. The disaster of Vietnam flowed right out of the Gulf of Tonkin Resolution that most people now admit was adopted by Congress based on reports of an attack on a U.S. patrol boat that did not happen.

NONSENSE BENEFICIARY. It would seem impossible that any American could have benefited from the Vietnam conflict. But remember: someone usually benefits from even the most horrid situation. Lyndon Johnson is a prime candidate for beneficiary, based on his own pathological perception of what made sense. But don't forget that the military-industrial complex doesn't have nearly as much to do during a prolonged outbreak of peace. Understandably, a lot of military types don't feel fulfilled without a taste of combat. The sting of battle is almost mandatory in the scheme of promotion to higher ranks. The Gulf of Tonkin Resolution had many fathers. However, a fully-operating Nonsense Test would have prevented a lot of its widows and orphans.

5. *NONSENSE: POISON APPLES.* The scientific knowledge we possess indicates that most of the carcinogens we encounter occur in nature. So let's take a look at the mob procedures by which we ban the use of chemicals. Sure, there are chemicals that should be kept miles away from people, but the absence of many chemical products would also mean a hungrier, less-healthy populace. The Alar apple scam is a pretty good example. The damage done by the Alar scare outweighed substantially its questionable benefits, least of all its actual ones. The scientific community wasn't nearly as impressed by that alleged threat to the public health as the movie stars and panic masters who ramrodded apples off the market.

The duty not to falsely yell "fire" in a crowded theater needs to be applied to most of these situations. Even if the Alar scare had been supported by solid scientific data, the terrified mother who sent the highway patrol to intercept the school bus to take the apple out of her child's lunch box was overwrought, wouldn't you say?

NONSENSE BENEFICIARY. The only apparent beneficiaries of this deal were cause addicts. The casualties were family farmers who lost it all. There was no pre-established group of poisoned apple watchdogs, so the leaders of the Alar scare seemed to be on loan from other national panic attacks. Presumably, they have returned to promoting their other long-term causes.

6. *NONSENSE: THE HOMELESS.* During the Carter administration, in the name of humanitarianism, the mentally ill were "deinstitutionalized." That is, they were tossed out into the street.

NONSENSE BENEFICIARY. A beneficiary for this shenanigan is hard to find. At the time, no constituency existed for the "homeless." So it is hard to imagine who would argue that life on the street is kinder than life in the institution other than someone who had never been in either place. This might be an example of advocating change as an exercise in power. It could be the action of guilt mongers or the devotees of chaos. Or was it a mindless attack on the status quo by some causies who were between engagements?

But there is another explanation; a sinister one. Mental health is a multi-billion dollar industry.

These are just a few examples of Nonsense Testing. Some

beneficiaries are obvious, while for some, the profit motive is better concealed. But gullibility is not a survival skill. A society in which citizens unquestioningly accept the dictates of a suspect evening news or the allegations of movie star "crossover experts" is no freer than one whose people are told what to think by an unelected leader who owns the newspapers.

Most movements do not start with a proven fact and then develop a philosophy and enlist dedicated workers. Rather, movements originate with a wish or prejudice. It is then shrouded in mysticism, enhanced by movie stars and rock and roll, and sold to a huge populace whose last cause has just dried up.

Most of us have fallen in love with a used sports car or some other bit of frippery and have abandoned all willingness to see the obvious because we wanted it so badly. But let's apply the same skepticism to all movements and causes that we apply to used car salesmen and religious hucksters. Or for that matter, let's treat them as presumptive liars until they have passed the Nonsense Test.

PRACTICE NONSENSE TEST

Just like you used to do in school, apply the Nonsense Test to something you have heard or read recently.

If the assertion doesn't pass the Nonsense Test, write down the name of the person who told you it was God's own truth.

Remember him the next time he tries to sell you an ideological used car.

If the Beneficiary you identify doesn't include "the public, decent folks everywhere, our country, world peace, common decency" and the like, you already know the answer. Be tough in applying the test. Presume the story is being told to you by your brother-in-law and require him to prove his contention before you loan him the money.

Better still, let's try treating all the people who are peddling ideas as though they were the Devil. We all know enough not to believe him. So let's not be persuaded until a goodly number of angels say he's telling the truth.

And remember, the Devil is the world's best teller of lovely stories.

Chapter 27

The Devil

What will the preachers do when the Devil is saved?
—Brother Dave Gardner

Eric Hoffer, the longshoreman philosopher, once observed "It is startling to see how the oppressed almost invariably shape themselves in the image of their hated oppressors. That the evil men do lives after them is partly due to the fact that those who have reason to hate the evil most shape themselves after it and thus perpetuate it."

If he had visited this country in the Nineteen Sixties and had returned now, Pogo Possum would once again observe "We have met the enemy and he is us." But now, the heirs of The Movement look just like the enemy we fought. For a few vivid examples of how well we learned the lessons of our oppressors, try these:

BACK THEN	TODAY
• Los Angeles race riots	• Los Angeles race riots
• Sen. Joe McCarthy	• Politically Correct thought

• Blacklisting	• Blacklisting
• Lying about Vietnam	• Lying about affirmative action
• Official racial bias	• Official reverse bias
• Elitism	• Elitism
• Establishment fascism	• Liberal fascism
• *Ad infinitum*	• *Ad infinitum*

The basic premise of The Movement was that Lyndon Johnson, Richard Nixon, the government, the college dean, university administrations and anyone over 30 were all the Devil. In the case of the universities, it wasn't that they were forcing fascist philosophy down our throats. But we felt they acted like fascists in keeping us from doing what we were supposedly in school for—to question, to explore, to participate in the clash of ideas. Unofficial campus newspapers were banned, off-campus newspapers were banned, on-campus free-speech forums were regulated to death, and every official campus newspaper had a faculty censor sitting atop the printing press. We felt the First Amendment was being held prisoner.

MEKONG DELTA

The government, however, went even further. They cut the First Amendment right out of the Constitution. If they didn't like what we said about the Vietnam War and how we demonstrated our opposition, we magically became classified 1-A for the military draft, and suddenly would find ourselves in the Mekong Delta looking for land mines with our feet.

Going directly from campus to combat was a pretty stiff price for expressing opinions American revolutionary Thomas Paine would have considered too routine to mention. In the Nineteen Sixties, the bottom line was that the government and the universities effectively suspended the Constitution of the United States in an attempt to control what people would think by controlling what they could say and do.

Well, here we are again. Lyndon Johnson could hire most of today's professional liberals as consultants on suppression of free speech. They have forgotten that the purpose of the First Amendment is to protect unpopular speech—stuff that is really offensive, that is so disagreeable we can't even bear to hear it. Speech that attacks who we are and what we stand for. Likewise, it is our right not to listen to ideas that we do not like and to condemn them soundly.

Today, however, the liberal Democrats have taken a quantum jump in oppressive behavior—Politically Correct thought. The more the Politically Correct extend their right to do and say what they want, the more they limit those rights for people they disagree with

LITTLE BLACK SAMBO AND THE COMMUNISTS

At the University of Texas, two incidents occurred during the same week in April 1990. Members of a fraternity donned T-shirts with the representation of a Fiji Islander, which had once been their mascot. The mascot resembled Little Black Sambo. Elsewhere on campus, a self-proclaimed atheist-Communist group burned the American flag.

After substantial black-led protest, the fraternity was thrown off campus, then required by the university to do 1,200 hours of minority-oriented community service. The members were required to submit to minority-oriented "reeducation" through 1994.

As to the flag-burners who committed a felony, the university did nothing.

Both actions involved Constitutionally protected free speech. Both actions offended the hell out of most observers. Why was the offense to the black community treated so differently from the offense to all Americans who wish not to see the flag defiled? The idea of forced "reeducation" camps sounds like Mao's China and Pol Pot's Cambodia. But this was not China. This was not Cambodia. This was Austin, Texas.

If forced reeducation is a good idea for the racially insensitive who violated no law, shouldn't it also be applied to the patriotically insensitive who did break the law?

Free speech did not become a root of our culture because it

appears in the Constitution. It is in the Constitution because it is a root of our culture.

Without free speech, American culture as we know it simply could not exist. The average American adult would not recognize an America without a First Amendment. Of all the cultural foundations upon which our nation rests, the right to speak freely is the one upon which every other freedom rests.

This is not a matter of law; it is a matter of how we think and feel. There is a built-in agreement among most of us that the next guy should get to say his piece, even if we totally disagree with it.

SACRED COWS

By way of horrible example, the University of Michigan, Duke, Stanford, Emory and a couple of hundred other colleges have actually passed regulations that lead to expulsion of any students who speak derogatorily about women, minorities, gays, the disabled and other victim groups. Two people sharing a tasteless joke about one of these sacred cows would be wise to speak in whispers and to be very careful whom they share it with. Does that sound a bit like old East Germany? How about the USSR? Does that sound like the late, crazy U.S. Sen. Joe McCarthy and the Commie-hunting House Un-American Activities Committee? Haven't we learned anything?

FIRST AMENDMENT HEROES

Fortunately, some genuine First Amendment heroes and some federal judges have recognized the similarities. But this stuff still goes on at American universities. Unless we look back with warm fondness on the blacklisting of the Nineteen Fifties, we had better put a stop to all this.

Remember the words of Rev. Martin Niemoeller, a German Lutheran minister, arrested by the Gestapo in 1938. He was freed from Dachau concentration camp in 1945 by Allied forces.

In Germany, the Nazis first came for the Communists, and I didn't speak up because I wasn't a Communist. Then they came for the Jews, and I didn't speak up because I wasn't Jewish. Then they came for the trade unionists, and I didn't speak up because I wasn't a trade unionist. Then they came for the Catholics, and I didn't speak up because I was a Protestant. Then they came for me, and by that time there was no one left to speak for me.

That happened only fifty years ago. What we are witnessing in Bosnia, Rwanda and Haiti must remind us that human nature hasn't really changed much.

Now, college students are routinely asserting that the First Amendment really shouldn't protect someone whose remarks make another student feel racially uncomfortable. Are these scholars' political science and ethics professors still cashing their paychecks? There are some basic rights that cannot be sacrificed to any goal, regardless how noble or humane it purports to be.

HOME-GROWN FASCISTS

If you need a label to describe this phenomenon, there is one with a long history: fascism. Fascism occurs in a culture for several reasons. A dictator who wants to tell people what to do at gunpoint is a fascist whether he has ever read a book on the subject or not. The nature of fascism doesn't change just because he uses something more subtle than a gun to enforce his will. Fear of economic reprisal and social pressure have kept more people enslaved than the barrel of a gun.

Lyndon Johnson's generation fought and died against the evils of Nazi Germany, Fascist Italy and the Empire of Japan. Yet as Eric Hoffer observed, when the chips were down, that generation, victorious over fascism, adopted the tactics they had hated yet learned so well. America in the Nineteen Sixties cannot be compared to the era of *Der Fuhrer, Il Duce* and Gen. Hideki Tojo. But you don't have to adopt everything someone stands for to pick up a few of his most offensive practices.

Look around today. Are the Clintonistas any kinder to those who offend the Politically Correct than LBJ and the universities were to the students of the Nineteen Sixties?

TOUGH QUESTIONS

Leftist America has created a litany of things that are not okay to say and a host of tough questions that are simply unaskable. Does that sound like your hopes and dreams for America? Don't we have a duty to make our country safe for people who want to call each other hateful names, just as we worked hard to make it safe for people with different views of how to live their lives?

Do the "kind intentions" of the elitist make him any less an elitist—a person who believes he knows what is best for us and is willing to enforce his will by force?

If you could hold a convention of all sorts of elitists and keep the lights down low, black Muslim Louis Farrakhan and the Grand Wizard would make a date to get together next time they were in town.

PEOPLE LIKE US

A dictator who makes you do something that is good for you at the point of a gun is no less a threat to your liberty than the dictator who does something bad to you with that same gun. Suspending the First Amendment is no less ominous just because the dictator is a good fellow.

The First Amendment was designed to protect the rest of the people from people like us.

CHAPTER 28

THE END OF LET'S PRETEND

America is not a gift. It must be earned by each generation after generation. It must be recreated by every member of each generation. If not, it all will be lost. Forever.

—The Author

Since World War II, the United States has experienced a prosperity like nothing ever seen by humanity. We live longer, we eat better, and we possess more stuff than any culture in history. In fact, we have done so well that we have forgotten the primary lesson of nature and history: everything has a price tag.

We didn't even recognize the biggest price tag of all because we mistook it for a benefit. We became removed from the demands of survival. We smoked, we drank, we ate rich foods, we threw garbage all over our land, and we knew we would live forever.

Our food indulgence got to us first. Our arteries clogged up, our blood pressure soared, and we couldn't walk up a flight of stairs without gasping. So we became health nuts. We jogged, we exercised, we ate yogurt, we rebuked red meat and became healthier. We actually learned from our bad experiences.

Mistreatment of the environment got us next. Crude oil covered our beaches, acid rained into our lakes and forests, the air became unfit for human consumption, and pollution darked the sun. So we became environmentalists. We sorted our trash, passed laws, drove more efficient cars, picketed polluters and, ever so gradually, patient Earth began to respond. We actually learned from our bad experiences.

Then came our most perilous experience of all. We ignored the wisdom of our fathers, tinkered with our Constitution, abandoned our sovereign borders, turned our backs on what made us great, and forgot that we are all Americans. We tolerated quotas, bowed to the ringmasters of divisiveness, suspended the rules of reason, and became a land of *Let's Pretend*. The survival of the American culture itself came to peril. And then, and then? And then we did nothing. We learned nothing at all from our bad experiences. Or did we?

Why We Did It

Why did we do all of these things to ourselves? Simple: we did it because it felt good! From spoiled Nineteen Sixties children, we became a self-indulgent adult majority. Yet we have shown an amazing willingness to whip ourselves into shape, paying the price for healthier bodies and a more livable environment, because we love ourselves that much. We have noticed that staying in touch with our physical survival makes sense. We have only one major job left to assure our survival: the reclaiming of the American common culture.

We seem to have overlooked that the health spa, organic vegetables and low-emission automobiles are almost entirely a function of the world we live in—not the world everyone else lives in. Only in America are we rich enough to be so concerned about ozone levels, rather than how to get enough food to feed our families day to day. Nowhere else in the civilized world can so much attention be paid to such values—not in England, not in Sweden, not anywhere.

THE FULCRUM OF DISASTER

But in the United States, we are running on cultural momentum. Culture is designed to insure survival, so it should not seem strange that culture itself is based on survival—just as nature is. Since the end of World War II, we have seen some refinements to our culture; the rise of fair play as a governing principle, and out of that, equality of opportunity.

We have also witnessed the shifting fulcrum of cultural balance—one that is the harbinger of cultural disaster—the shift from equal opportunity to guaranteed equal outcome. This last change is to the survival of the American people and culture what overpopulation is to the Earth itself. It has the same basic cause, too—

self-indulgence. Are we willing to make the same sacrifices to save Life Boat America as we are to lower our cholesterol and to curb smokestack emissions? Have we finally figured out the connection between saving American culture and saving everything else we hold sacred? Are we ready to return to survival and fair play as our guiding principles?

No one says this will be easy. We will be forced to slaughter a whole herd of our most favored liberal sacred cows—affirmative action, social promotion, racial preferences—as well as the taste of the liberal elitists for imposing their will on the rest of us. We must put liberal fascism up against the wall.

If we do, the payoff will be a leaner, survival-based nation in which all of us can live in health, freedom and safety.

The prescription for what ails us is simple—the once and future American common culture itself. So what does this mean to us? It means we will all speak a common language and treat one another the same, regardless of how badly our group may have been treated before we were born. No preferences, no easy fixes, no exemptions from the First Amendment. It means equality of opportunity, coupled with the right to succeed or fail based on our own hard work and abilities. It means building upon our similarities rather than glorifying our differences. It means the realization of Dr. King's dream—that each of us will be judged by the content of our character, not the color of our skin. It means we as a nation will actually stand for what we have been saying for a long time that we stand for. What do you think? Does this sound like an America you would like to live in?

What will we have if we let go of *Let's Pretend?* Survival, pure and simple. We will become a country, a nation, able to handle whatever comes our way, from within or without.

THE COMMON GOOD

We will also foster a culture that can change as it needs to, incorporating the strengths of new blood while being capable of rejecting nonsense wrapped in the camouflage of cultural mysticism. Americans will be encouraged to be themselves while still being expected to pull for the common good—the very good that allows us to be ourselves. We will adapt quickly enough to stay alive and responsive, while knowing when to "just say no" to cultural fads that have so damaged this nation.

There will be hazards. While our friends across the old Iron Curtain have had a big enough dose of socialism to reject the concept, we may still be tempted to lie about human nature and tinker with the economic and social marketplace. While Eastern Europeans were fighting for their survival daily, we grew fat and complacent in our abandonment of survival. If socialism were the answer to mankind's problems, the East Germans would be painting the Berlin Wall instead of selling its pieces in souvenir shops. There is a powerful likelihood that an elitist liberal Congress hasn't learned the lessons of survival and has more horrendous social-engineering experiments ready to spring on us. Sen. Barry Goldwater reminded us, after all, that a government big enough to give us everything we want is also powerful enough to take everything we have. An overwhelming example is the Clintons' health care plan that will confiscate one-seventh of the economy from private hands, moving it to government control.

MID-LIFE CRISIS

And that brings us to the job that we all have to do. The Nineteen Nineties are a decade of mid-life crisis for the nation, not just for the Boomers. But we will all be needed to take back our birthright, regardless of our generation, and particularly the young people of our nation. Now is the time to take a close look at what we have wrought. It is also the time to ask ourselves some Tough Questions. "What is it all about? What have we accomplished? Was it all worth it? What should we have done differently?" And "How do we clean up the mess we have made?" Simply asking a few polite and sensitive questions won't do it. Powerful people and forces have a huge interest in keeping some of us dependent and angry and the rest of us docile and gullible. They won't give up without a fight.

So where do we start?

There are city council members out there who need to know how we feel. Your congressman may be unresponsive, but he knows there are more of us than there are of him. Your fellow citizens need to know they are not alone—that you are as fed up with liberal fascism as they are.

THIS IS AMERICA

Let them know what you think of *Let's Pretend*. Let your university know what you think of liberal fascist repression of free speech at your alma mater. Start talking to your neighbors. Run for the school board. Run for city council. Run for the legislature. Run for the very halls of Congress itself. If you can't run, back somebody who will force the issue by asking tough questions. Don't allow the candidates to play *Let's Pretend*. Things don't have to stay the way they have been—this is America. We've always known how to change.

At the same time, let's show some compassion. Most leaders of *Let's Pretend* aren't thugs. Some are decent people who may be as ready as we are to pull the plug on this horrible social experiment. Playing *Let's Pretend* is just their job. Give them the same chance to see the light as you would ask for yourself. This is America. There is room for us all, even for folks who were dead wrong and damned stubborn about admitting it.

By the same token, don't expect entrenched vested interests

to give up without a battle. Look how long it took for Eastern Europe to overthrow a system based on a faulty view of how people really are and how things really work. Keep the heat on them—be tough but reasonable. The goal is worth it. American citizens can be restored to the dignity they deserve. Hard work can make a difference. People can truly be judged on the content of their character. This is America.

Remember that the great civilizations of Rome and Egypt, surprisingly enough, were open cultures. But there was a price tag. To be a Roman or an Egyptian, their new citizens were expected to speak and live the culture of their land.

THE CURE

If we can learn these lessons, we can bring about the end of *Let's Pretend*. But having diagnosed the disease is not enough. We have to undo our debilitating case of touchy-feely sensitivity that demands that we tolerate the intolerable, and has reduced our standards to zero. We have to roll up our sleeves, be willing to endure some tough, stinging criticism, and get on with the cure. The therapy for counteracting liberal fascism needs a name.

Let's call it Insensitivity Training.

And it starts with all of us getting used to asking and hearing what can only be called Tough Questions.

CHAPTER 29

INSENSITIVITY TRAINING

*After years of work and therapy, we are finally so
sensitive to one another's feelings that we can't even
talk to each other.*

—The Author's Sensitivity Trainer

*Yeah! We've made a growth industry out of getting
our feelings hurt.*

—The Author

I spend a lot of time talking to all kinds of groups—civic,
business, student, political—you name it. I even show up in the
newspapers once in a while. I try to shoot straight on touchy
issues. My friend Dwight thinks the only reason my house hasn't
been burned down is that the folks who would be most offended
by my observations have no one to read the newspaper to them.
That sounds a little cynical, but what he said made me think. As
Americans, even when we say we are telling the truth, we are
always ducking a lot of Tough Questions. When we did the final
edit on this book, I had to decide how much truth is really safe to
tell. Am I really up to asking all of the Tough Questions?

I don't necessarily mean questions that are hard or important or even confusing, although they are often all three. A Tough Question is a question you don't ask without first looking around to see if "one of them" is in the room, whoever "them" happens to be. It's the question that makes your stomach jump when you hear someone else ask it. It is the question that can call down upon your head the latest trendy liberal indictment: insensitivity.

TOUGH QUESTION SAFETY ZONE

A couple of years ago, I gave a talk to a bunch of business people and invited them to propose their own Tough Questions. We designated the room a "Tough Question Safety Zone"—anything goes, no one gets mad and, most important, no answers allowed. We would be practicing how to ask Tough Questions, not how to answer them. Answers would come later. I told the audience to get their own Tough Questions ready. They were the ones who needed loosening up—not me.

One sweet lady volunteered quickly, "Why can't we all live together in peace and harmony?" Sweet, but nobody flinched. Not a Tough Question.

A guy scanned the room nervously and whispered "Do men with toupees really think we don't notice?" The crowd cringed and heads swiveled. My point was made that Tough Questions don't have to be important—just uncomfortable. Then the questions began to flow.

"If Jesse Jackson can say 'my people,' can Ross Perot say 'you people'?" "If women really don't want to be considered sex objects, who reads all that soft-core pornography in Cosmopolitan?" "Why are there so few Asians at the welfare office?"

They were getting the hang of it.

"Do fat women in white stretch pants own mirrors?" "Why does the Virgin Mary's face keep showing up on shower curtains and backyard toolsheds?"

"All right!" I said.

A woman lawyer asked "If Magic Johnson is a hero and role model, what does that make all the people he slept with and probably infected?" Someone blurted out a graphic response.

"No answers!" I shouted.

They yelled back: "Why isn't it racist to say honkie or gringo?" "If it's not OK to say Chinaman, what do we call an Englishman?" They were rolling. "If you can inherit your parents' looks and talent, what about their dull wits and criminal tendencies?" "How come Murphy Brown never has any 14-year-old crack mothers on her show?"

I FEEL YOUR PAIN

A liberal was howling in pain, so I popped the conservatives: "How many people at an anti-abortion rally have adopted a crack baby?" The liberals cheered. The pro-lifers scowled. Someone yelled "Why do homosexuals talk that way?" He hit a nerve. "Since a lot more people die from cancer and heart disease, why do we put all the money into AIDS?" He hit the nerve again.

"When are the Japanese going to pay reparations for Pearl Harbor?" "Who is the racist when black Africans kill each other?" "Ouch!" I said. "If affirmative action is such a great idea, where are all the white basketball players in the NBA?" Tempers were getting touchy. "What's the difference between Geraldo Rivera and any other pimp?" Everybody laughed.

An eternity of questions poured out. "If it's OK to have a Miss Black Houston contest that no whites can enter . . ." An embarrassed black businessman stood up, gritted his teeth and completed the question. A successful-looking Hispanic asked "If an illegal alien is an undocumented worker, is a burglar an undocumented tenant?" A woman shouted "Is having more kids than you can feed any better than starving them intentionally?"

Hands were waving. The genie was out of the bottle.

ROBBER BARONS

"If women really do top-quality work for a fraction of men's wages, why don't the robber barons fire all their men and quadruple their profits?" "If this is such a rotten, racist country, why do more people break in than sneak out?" A wild-eyed looking guy shouted, "Is your house made out of wood and where is it?"

It sounded like a pretty good time to leave, but the Tough Questions idea had developed a life of its own. My first experiment with Insensitivity Training was a success. All I had to do was keep yelling "No answers! No answers! For right now, all we want are the Tough Questions."

No fists were swung and people were still shouting Tough Questions as I left. I declared the whole evening a victory. Driving home, I surveyed my findings. There are a lot of really serious questions in America that aren't being asked. So how will we get the answers? That is probably the toughest question we need to ask and the one we had better deal with first.

I recalled that most of the Tough Questions my audience asked dealt with things that divide us—gender, race, sexual orientation, criminality, welfare, illegal immigration, culture and ethics. Things—tragically—that we have let so-called liberal leaders make taboo for honest discussion. How in the hell will we ever get the honest answers we desperately need if we can't even talk to each other for fear of hurting someone's feelings?

WHERE TO START

So where do we start? After the meeting, a man told me "I've got a lifetime full of Tough Questions." I suspected that we all did. So I wrote an article for The Houston Post about Insensitivity Training, asking the readers to send me their Tough

Questions. In the weeks that followed, readers sent hundreds of Tough Questions. And then I took the Tough Questions show on the road. I talked to another group, then two, then more. Everywhere I went, the same questions came up over and over. People were burning with questions they had been afraid to ask.

SOMETHING AMAZING

Then something truly amazing happened. People from the groups I had talked to began to call. They had started holding their own Tough Questions meetings—in the coffee room, at home, wherever. And out of it all something wonderful had begun to happen—they had started talking to one another, honestly and openly. They began to discover that they shared the same fears and the same hopes, the same failures and the same dreams. Black, white, brown and yellow—they started seeing each other as friends and equals. Rich and poor talked about their hopes for their children. Unwed mothers and religious zealots talked about education and safety in their schools. Bosses had the chance to find out what their employees really cared about and how they could work together for their common good. Moms and dads had family Tough Questions sessions. One mother with tears in her eyes told me how she and her teenage daughter had become friends again when she made it safe for her daughter to ask her own personal Tough Questions. I heard that story again and again.

Do Try This at Home

I know that you have your own Tough Questions and you need someplace safe to ask them. So do your friends and neighbors. Get together with them and try this out. Remember the rules: 1) Only questions; 2) No answers for now; 3) If it doesn't make your stomach jump, it isn't really a Tough Question; 4) Don't get mad; 5) Respect the other guy's Tough Question as much as you do your own; 6) Do it in small doses; and 7) Quit before there is bloodshed. Oh yes! Once you get comfortable with the process, be sure to include some folks who don't usually see things your way. But go slowly until you get the hang of it. Have some fun in the process. Remember that a sense of humor can take the sharp edge off things.

This is not an invitation to drag out the old "let it all hang out, truth at any price" malarkey. The purpose of Tough Questions is not to hurt and wound. The purpose is to let us open up and start being honest with one another, particularly about things that can be painful. Any family counselor will tell you that as long as folks are talking openly, there is hope. This is just as true of the political and cultural mess we find our nation in as it is of a troubled family. But you have to approach the whole process thoughtfully and with mutual respect.

Help me out, as well. I am putting together a handbook for Insensitivity Training and I need your Tough Questions. Send them to me in care of my publisher, Commonwealth Publishing, Inc., Post Office Box 130946, Houston, Texas 77219. I will get our Tough Questions together and put them out there for the world to see. And once we get in some practice at asking and hearing Tough Questions, maybe we can start on the answers.

HATE PROFITEERS

Our Politically Correct critics may not like this kind of honest discussion, but it is a better approach than the ones they have been coming up with. People who make a handsome living peddling divisiveness have a lot to lose when we all start talking to one another and stop treating each other like enemies. But if there is one thing we can do to bring these hate profiteers to their knees, this is it.

After you get warmed up on your own Tough Questions, take a shot at those in the next chapter.

CHAPTER 30

TOUGH QUESTIONS

It is better to know some of the questions than all of the answers.

—James Thurber

BIG GOVERNMENT

- If the President can only hold office for eight years, why do we have to put up with congressmen forever?
- If you don't like the service at the Post Office, what do you expect from federal health care?
- If federal health care is such a great deal, how come congressfolks from Hawaii, California and New York want their constituents exempted from Clinton's health deal?
- Equal rights, affirmative action, OSHA and Social Security. If these laws are such great ideas for you and me, how come they don't apply to your congressman?
- Since your congressman can mail stuff to you without paying for the stamps, why can't you call him collect?

HOODLUMS

- Who really believes a 14-year-old killer is a child?
- If a kid pointing a gun at you doesn't get treated like an adult criminal, what will it take?
- Why are kids who are old enough to kill too young to be punished?

AFFIRMATIVE ACTION

- What do you really think of your affirmative action co-worker? Come on now, tell the truth.
- Can you really respect someone who demands a handout?
- Do minorities really need college entrance exams with training wheels on them?
- If minorities truly want control of their own destinies, are they willing to take responsibility for their own disasters?

ILLEGITIMACY

- Is there really a desperate shortage of illegitimate children in America?
- If we are really tired of criminals, why do we pay welfare mothers to have them?

WELFARE

- How many people have gotten enough welfare to make them

say "No thanks. That's enough for me!"?

- Since being on welfare is really a career choice, shouldn't we offer a college degree in it?

FAIR'S FAIR

- If pro-life folks can blockade abortion clinics, can atheists blockade churches?
- Why do we spend more per capita on AIDS than on heart disease, breast cancer or Alzheimer's?
- If we can have black pride week, can we have white pride week?
- If liberal Democrats can tell you not to smoke cigarettes at home, what can you forbid them to do in the privacy of their homes?

UNINVITED GUESTS

- Do we owe illegal aliens a free education?
- Do we owe them a free lunch?
- Why do we owe them anything at all?
- If we do have to educate every illegal kid in America, should we invade Mexico and open a preschool program?
- If breaking into our country won't get you put in jail, why should anything else?
- Why should the child of an immigration criminal receive the

greatest gift the U.S. can bestow—citizenship?

- If we have to give people money, can we make them ask for it in our own language?

TOWER OF BABEL

- If you don't have to speak English to vote, why don't we make Congress do business in Spanish every Tuesday?
- How can an Asian immigrant learn to speak better English than an inner-city black who was born here?

HYPOCRISY

- How many liberals have a family of illegal aliens residing in their extra bedroom?
- Why don't liberals put a sign in their yard that says "Hot Meals, Clean Towels, and Free Bathroom Privileges for the Homeless!"?
- Is freezing to death on the street more humane than eating a hot meal in a mental hospital?
- How many white liberals have moved into a poor black neighborhood to serve as role models?
- When do you expect to see Hillary Clinton get a Pap smear at a public health clinic?
- Why is public school not good enough for Chelsea Clinton or 40% of congressmen's kids?

- If students can't pray in school, why do prisoners get to become Muslims and order from the special menu?
- How should an alcohol-addicted officeholder vote on a law to legalize marijuana?
- How should an officeholder who uses marijuana vote on a law to legalize marijuana?
- If liberals want to see a more diverse Congress, why don't half the Democrats quit and hand over their jobs to black women?

NATIONAL DEFENSE

- Do you really think the Soviet Union folded up because they were afraid of Teddy Kennedy?

FEMINISM

- How exactly did Princess Diana and Hillary Clinton get their jobs?
- If feminists believe in equality, why do they need so many laws to keep their feelings from getting hurt?
- Do you understand that Bill Clinton's girlfriends have much more corroboration for their stories than Anita Hill had for hers?
- How much breast cancer research money should we spend on AIDS instead?

PET PROJECTS

- Have you noticed that AIDS isn't really everyone's disease?
- If kids don't imitate what they see on television, how come TV stations have advertising departments?

CRIME

- Does the sad childhood of the guy who killed you make you any less dead?
- Would you rather have an addict kill you to get money for his fix, or purchase his supplies cheaply at the pharmacy?
- If poverty is what causes crime, why did Americans obey the law during the Great Depression?
- Do liberals feel sorry for bigots because they had a deprived childhood?
- If you were a criminal, would you turn in your gun for a pair of basketball tickets?
- What's wrong with bread and water?
- How come a military tent is good enough for patriots but not nice enough for criminals?
- How much cable TV does the Constitution really guarantee a convicted killer?
- How many poor kids would a liberal Democrat be willing to starve to keep one convicted killer alive?

Tough questions!

CHAPTER 31

AMERICA: AN OWNER'S MANUAL

This land is your land. This land is my land.
—Woody Guthrie

When someone asks you what you learned from reading this book, tell them you found out what is wrong with America and what we can do about it. Tell them you know fourteen steps that can put our country back on track, that can reverse our nation's long slide into Democrat Dependency Syndrome. Here they are.

CONGRESS

1. Term Limits. Our problem is not just that we pay our congressmen too much, it is what they do when they show up for work. Make them go home sooner. Impose term limits without exception.

Senators can serve two terms. If they can't put their personal mark on America in twelve years, another 100 years won't help.

Representatives can serve only eight years. Four terms is

enough time for them to prove whatever point they promised their voters they would make.

If they won't take the term-limits pledge, don't vote for them. Warn your neighbors. Just like Paul Revere. "The vultures are coming! The vultures are coming!"

2. Pensions. Cut off their fancy retirement plan. Let them collect social security, just like you and I hope to do. Or better yet, let them learn how to save for a rainy day. Practicing thrift will have a wonderful effect on the respect they show for the money you and I give our government.

3. Medical Benefits. Throw every one of them out of Bethesda Naval Hospital, one of the finest medical institutions in the world. Let them call their family doctor and sit in the waiting room, just like you and I do. Or better yet, let them go to the same public health clinic where Hillary Clinton gets her checkup.

4. Obey the Law. Make them obey every law you and I have to. Right now, they can discriminate against minorities when they hire their overpaid staffs. They don't have an OSHA inspector telling them limousine rides are bad for their backs. They don't have to pay women the same wages as men. They don't have to hire their helpers without regard to their race, creed, religion, or sexual orientation. Unlike us, they don't have to hire the blind as proofreaders or the quadriplegic as tap dancers.

Before they can pass a new tax, apply it to their paychecks

for a one-year trial period. When they discover how much even damn good laws can hurt the lonely taxpayer or small business-man, they might think twice before they pass the really silly ones.

UNINVITED GUESTS

5. The Borders. Seal the borders, now. Build a wall and use the military, but stop the flow of illegal immigrants today. Make all newcomers to our country play by the same rules as the legal immigrants who turn into such good citizens. When your liberal neighbor says the U.S. military has no business patrolling our borders, ask him what the Army Corps of Engineers is doing deciding which of our natural creeks and streams would look better lined with concrete. If the Army can change the course of rivers, they can certainly block the tidal wave of the uninvited. They're engineers, aren't they?

If we really need a million illiterate Guatemalan peasants a year to keep the wheels of industry turning, make them play by the rules.

Put a gate in the wall across our southern border. Let the Mexican government build a nice hospitality center on their side. To get to our side, each applicant has to stand in line and say "Hello. My name is Juan Ortega. I thank you for letting me into your wonderful country. I will do my best to obey your laws and not be more trouble than I am worth. Here is my forwarding address." When their first contact with this country demonstrates our regard for our own laws, they may be inclined to treat the blessings of the U.S. with more respect.

Don't give me that picking on Latinos look, either. The same rules apply to those pesky Canadians who are fleeing from the benefits of Clinton-style socialized medicine. And if you want to find a Pakistani or an Asian on a snowmobile headed south without a green card, Moose Jaw, Saskatchewan, is a good place to start looking.

6. Deportation. Round up the current crop of illegal residents and deport them. Sounds tough? "But they are already here," the liberal whiners will whine, of course.

Yet even the most dithering of liberals encountering a burglar in their house would ask him to leave, even if he has his pregnant wife and eleven kids helping sort the silverware. Just because someone has started a big family based on being a crook doesn't make it OK.

7. Free Lunch. Shut down public assistance, welfare, food stamps and Medicaid for every person who has broken into this country. Some of their children may be citizens and we may owe them an education, but we don't have to take care of their parents.

8. Born Here. Amend the Fourteenth Amendment to the Constitution that says if mama can run the 100-yard dash across the border just as her labor pains kick in, the result is a citizen. The purpose served by that provision has long since run out. Keeping it on the books is just an invitation to the pregnant to climb over the fence.

¿SAY WHAT?

9. U.S. English. Make standard American English the law of the land. Speaking a foreign language is wonderful and uplifting, but every government form and ballot must be in English. Once the border is sealed, the pressure to give criminals money and services in a foreign language will ease up a lot.

10. Bilingual Education. Easy. Stop bilingual education, immediately. For students who have a right to free schooling, replace bilingual education with one year of total-immersion training in standard American English. Kids learn languages very easily. At the end of one year, any student who can't speak English can be placed in special classes for the learning disabled. As for the bilingual teachers who can't speak English and who purchased fake diplomas to go to work for the Houston Independent School District, they can study English in jail.

SCHOOL

11. Affirmative Action. Choose teachers by color-blind evaluation. All teachers, regardless of race, who can't make the

WHERE LIBERALS GO TO DIE

cut can seek work where they can't hurt the children.

12. Social Promotions. If a kid can't or won't pass, flunk him.

Generations of American kids busted their butts for fear of not making it to the next grade with their classmates. If it worked then, it will work now.

13. One, Two and Three Strikes. Set up alternative schools run by retired drill sergeants that teach the three R's, basic survival skills and civics.

When a kid shows up in class with a gun or knife or hits a teacher, he has had his one strike. Off to educational reform school.

When a kid curses a teacher, disrupts a class or hits another student, he gets two strikes. Explain the short-sightedness of his current career plan and ship him out the next time he tries it.

When a kid refuses to study and gets in the way of those who do want to learn, he gets two rounds of counseling. Then off to the other place.

WHAT TO DO AFTER SCHOOL

14. National Service. Every young person will, sooner or later, turn 18, graduate from high school or drop out. The minute any of these events occurs, they head off for National Service. Two months of basic training will be followed by several months of contributing to America.

WHAT ABOUT US?

All of these changes will mean nothing if they don't also come from our hearts. Each of us has to sacrifice something that is special to us. Just like Lent. If you are a sports fan, start by refusing to attend a basketball game starring a player who has made a trip through drug rehab.

If you are a yuppie parent, refuse to hire an illegal nanny. Hire one of your countrymen who needs the work and pay him a fair wage. If you can't afford it, decide whether you really need that extra kid you are planning.

If you are a voyeur, peek through the keyhole of your own bedroom. Quit giving money to the sponsors of Geraldo Rivera, Phil Donahue and the rest of the toilet-bowl journalists.

If you like filthy language, teach your spouse how to cuss. Don't listen to shock jock Howard Stern or watch movies that think the average American learned to speak English in a whorehouse.

Take this chapter to every meeting where a candidate for anything is going to talk. Pick out the items that are relevant to the particular culprit and ask him where he stands. Don't let him wiggle. If he says he agrees with you, make him put it in writing. Round up a couple of witnesses, too.

The politicians may hate to see you coming. But we will all be better off if they have to keep their heads down and their stories straight.

ACKNOWLEDGMENTS

This book of observations, opinions and of my own view of the world was shaped by everything I have read and experienced and by thousands of people whose thoughts have influenced me. Trying to figure out exactly who should be credited for what is impossible. But if others' words and thoughts have become my own, I thank them now and promise to heartily acknowledge any sources who bring their contributions to my attention. I regret that I never met the late Eric Hoffer, whose insights on human behavior inspire my belief that we can clean this mess up.

My special thanks go to my wife, Linda Arlene, for her sense of history and nature. To my friend, Dwight W. Short, for his carefully-crafted advice and persistent encouragement whenever the dream would slip from my grasp. To Dale Johnson, whose gleeful laughter encouraged me to shoot big and wide.

I am deeply grateful to my old friend Connie Haywood of Gateway Graphics, and artist Jimmy deGuzman, who turned a flickering idea into the cover of this book. My thanks go to Craig O. Smith who refused to let the computers play *Let's Pretend*. Thanks to my classmate, Les Hewitt, for his legal advice. I also thank each of the volunteer readers who helped keep me from getting so close to the job as to lose my perspective. To my long-suffering staff, Nannette and Jodi, what can I say? Thanks.

And in the nick of time, arrived my uncommon friend, Rosie Walker, style book and red pencil in hand. The birth of this book was my personal rebirth. Rosie was the midwife.

I have written that Sgt. John Dred was one of the two best teachers I ever had. The other is Lester C. Coleman. Thanks, Les.

My final thank-you goes to those who served as horrible examples, both sincere and otherwise, who moved me to write this book. They know their names.

James T. Evans
Houston, Texas
July 1994

ABOUT THE AUTHOR

Lawyers are people who spend one-third of their lives getting a license to practice law and the rest of it looking for a book to write. This is that book.

—The Author

James T. Evans was born in 1943 and graduated *cum laude* from the University of Houston Law Center in 1968. While Evans was president of the University of Houston student body, he traveled throughout the United States, Mexico and Central America advising student leaders on takeovers of university administrations, management of protests, civil rights actions and seizing rights for students. He was jailed in Houston during student uprisings at Texas Southern University in 1967. He worked with national student protest leaders and campus radicals.

Together with the Quakers and other student leaders, Evans filed suit in 1967 against the Selective Service System and its director, Gen. Lewis B. Hershey. The suit resulted in draft protesters no longer being classified 1-A for burning their draft cards. He was lead counsel in federal cases establishing fundamental rights of conscientious objectors and reservists called to active duty against their will.

In 1968, Evans was an eyewitness when Federales in Mexico City opened fatal fire on student protesters and bystanders. In August of 1969, he was in Prague when Warsaw Pact tanks put down student demonstrations on the first anniversary of the overthrow of the Alexander Dubcek government and its Spring of Freedom. At age 26, Evans became the youngest judge in Texas. During the Nineteen Seventies, he served as a political consultant to liberal political campaigns.

During the administration of President Jimmy Carter, Evans came to sense the disastrous results of the liberal policies he had helped foment, particularly the relegation of black Americans to permanent underclass status to advance Democrat racial hegemony. After years of self-examination and what he calls Insensitivity Training, Evans is now a fully-recovered liberal.

In the Nineteen Sixties, Evans often visited a commune in the bohemian Montrose section of Houston known as Commonwealth House. Today, Commonwealth House is the Evans homestead. He is a Republican political strategist and chairman of a local draft board. His opinion pieces are seen in The Houston Post and the Houston Chronicle. He preaches a gospel of personal responsibility and dealing with Tough Questions to undo the disastrous influence of the Nineteen Sixties counter-culture.